APPROACHES TO ART

with this

[signature]

SOLVA

STAN ROSENTHAL:
APPROACHES TO ART

Stan Rosenthal

Shelagh Hourahane

GOMER

First Impression – 2002

ISBN 1 84323 115 8 (Hardback)
ISBN 1 84323 114 X (Softback)

Printed in Wales at
Gomer Press, Llandysul, Ceredigion

for
Nicola

CONTENTS

FOREWORD

If you look at enough art then reality can begin to take on some of that art's shape. It becomes stained by the artist's vision. A patina of what the painter has seen gets hung across your eyes. This is nowhere more evident than with landscape and especially in Pembrokeshire. This is the lost Wales of the far west where the light is like no other and the weather systems have their own unique mandates, it seems, from God. Here the great artists John Piper and Graham Sutherland used the forms they encountered, the shape of the horizons, the bend of the vegetation, the cast of the rocks and the darkness of the lanes to fill their paintings. Visiting Pembrokeshire now, everything has a haze of Sutherland and Piper across it. Things are no longer as they once were. Sutherland is inside them, Piper lies over them, changing their shape, the way the light strikes, morphing them into something different – perhaps into that which they always were.

So too with the work of Stan Rosenthal. If anyone in recent times has taken Pembrokeshire and possessed it, bent it to his vision, illuminated its colours, exposed its corners, changed the way it sits in the world, then it is him.

I've known Stan as a writer, zen master, painter, tai-chi teacher, businessman and down to earth human for decades. If he takes on a project then it will not flounder. Despite the odds it will always flourish. Pembrokeshire and its mellifluous landscape has reached inside Stan Rosenthal's spirit. From the small, almost photo-realistic work begun at Coedmor, near the Cardiganshire border, to the reductionist abstraction of the mustard and chrome-yellow 'Cliff' and 'Copse' series Pembrokeshire has become Stan.

He has always painted. At his rambling Cathedral Road, Cardiff house where I first knew him paintings occupied most of the wall space and were staked three deep in the hall. Stan was primarily a writer then – poetry, zen translations, art theory – but his brush never stopped moving. Later at Mabws Fawr, way north of the landsker, with its hand-crafted door architraves and its own cromlech out back erected by JCB, and now at Cowbridge where he presently lives, there are poems on scraps along the bookshelves. Notes in his back pocket. Drafts on his desk. Painting may predominate but Stan's pen is never still.

I head west to visit Nine Wells, a couple of miles along the coast from Stan's spiritual base at St Davids. Here at Aber Llong there have been massive landslips and great slabs of purple Caefai Sandstone lie faulted against the green-grey sandstones of the Solva Beds. The coastline has fallen into the sea like a row of books collapsing from an unstable shelf.

The blocks are vast and desperate in their weathered grit but the light from the west lifts them. I have no idea if Stan has ever painted here but looking at the landscape's mix of crush and angle, green and grey, growth and dissolution, it's as if he has. I'm seeing what Stan sees, some of it. I've become infected by his work.

PETER FINCH

A BIOGRAPHICAL STUDY

MOVING ON

The route to the Pembrokeshire coast has been followed by numerous artists, each choosing to meander along the county's high-hedged lanes in search of something personal and different, but all pulled by the particular character of the landscape and by its remarkable light. Stan Rosenthal made this journey about thirteen years ago, intending to explore the haunts of his precursors, Graham Sutherland and John Piper. In his turn he became a devotee of Wales's south-western fringe. However, the real story has to take us back through the skeins of a complex and fascinating life in order to discover what has contributed to the philosophy which lies behind his work as an artist and which affects the way that he looks at the landscape in which he now lives.

Stan Rosenthal's boyhood spent in the East End of London, and later south of the Thames, was a world far removed from the life that he was later to lead. His family, of East European Jewish origin, had migrated to what should have been a life free from threat and oppression. However, London in the 1930s had its share of anti-Semitic aggression and Stan, born in 1933, began life in one of the most uneasy and turbulent periods in our history. His early life was akin to that of many of his generation, undergoing the shock, anxiety and lack of comfort associated with the Second World War and especially the shattering attacks on the civilian population of the cities. In 1942, along with his sister and brother, Stan was evacuated out of London, leaving his own parents and being given a temporary home with a baker and his wife. He was nine years old at the time and it was as a part of this experience that he remembers feeling his first urge to draw. The baker started to make drawings to entertain and divert the child and, to his amazement, the little boy saw on the paper lines which transformed themselves into an elephant and a map. His childish mind identified with the magic of picture-making and he too wanted to be a 'draw-er'.

The post-war world continued to be a tough one for the lad who wanted only to be an artist. His story of conflict at home and of academic disinterest at school is not an unexpected one for a boy with his background who had discovered the creative path. For an artist from a working class and practical family, the ride is often a rough one. The story becomes even more familiar when at thirteen, Stan won a place at Southend College, where he could spend half the time studying art and the other half continuing with his general education. His father reluctantly agreed to let him attend the course on condition that he earned extra money to help support himself. Stan's studies included the traditional academic drawing from plaster casts of Roman sculptures, Lettering, Geometric Perspective Drawing, Oil and Watercolour Painting and Sculpture. Parental opposition to his chosen career continued, even when it could be seen that there were opportunities to be grasped in the post-war drive to equip Britain with a good teaching force. However, when the family moved to Leicester in 1950, Stan did join the Art College there and seemed to be set on an artistic career.

Always restless and inquisitive, Stan spent a lot of time away from college, earning money and making visits to the art galleries in London. There was a potent mix of paintings to be studied from within the English traditions of landscape, romanticism and painterliness. The artist remembers the landscape paintings of Cox and Cotman as early influences; he recalls that the work of William Blake and Samuel Palmer jointly provided lessons in expressing a deeply-felt spiritual view of the world, and that William Turner's paintings injected the energy associated with the bold use of colour. He also became familiar with twentieth-century artists, such as Henry Moore, Graham Sutherland and John Piper, who had pioneered new ways of looking at and of representing the world. When he looked at paintings by the Frenchman, Raoul Dufy, and later at the new colour field painting coming from the USA by Mark Rothko and others, he must have already recognised the potency of colour, line and shape, which was to contribute to his later work. There were anecdotal aspects to these visits to London. The most memorable arose from his exhibition as a pavement artist outside the Tate Gallery. The canvases placed against the railings in front of the gallery drew many interested gazes and some coins from pockets were placed in his imagined hat, drawn on the paving stones. Unknown to the young artist, one appreciative donor was Sir John Rothenstein, the Director of the Tate, who made some helpful comments about his work. When someone arrived with tea and biscuits for the surprised artist he discovered to whom he had been talking and that Sir John wanted to make a gesture of support for Stan's endeavour.

During the later 1940s and into the 1950s two quite different tendencies dominated the visual arts in Britain. Immediately after 1945 there was a sense that it was best to look inwards and to rediscover older traditions, which seemed to be particularly British. The neo-Romantic tendency included painters who admired the approach to landscape which had been demonstrated by some nineteenth-century artists, such as Samuel Palmer. It was in following a need to discover the past through present landscape, and to express a heightened emotional response to it, that a number of artists identified with the more remote parts of Britain, such as Pembrokeshire. A group of slightly younger artists responded to the post-war austerity and to the awareness of the strength of working people by favouring a type of realism which depicted ordinariness and even the drab quality of many people's lives, including those of most of the new generation of artists themselves.

Stan Rosenthal, poised at the beginning of a career as a painter, could have moved in either direction but he already admired the work of Graham Sutherland and John Piper, who were two of the leading neo-Romantics. Nevertheless, it was to be many years before Stan Rosenthal made his journey west, taking much the same road as they had travelled.

Rosenthal gained absolution from the experience of army life, into which most young men were conscripted for their National Service. He put up a successful case against the war in Korea that was then current and was allowed to remain at art college, agreeing that he would afterwards put in time doing work which was of public service. Stan Rosenthal reflects on the fact that the military authorities deemed him to be unsuitable for life in the army by recounting a story from much later in his life. He became Personal Assistant to a retired Brigadier General, who was Managing Director of INADCON, an International Advisory Consultancy in Behavioural Psychology. In conversation he learned that the Brigadier had selected Stan because he had not stood up to attention when he had entered the room where the candidates were gathered. However, at the time that he was an art student, fate intervened in the rather belligerent form of a duel and the eye injury incurred caused him to stop painting. This appeared to end his ambitions to be an artist and soon he undertook the community work which he had agreed to as an alternative to military service. As it had been suggested to him that he might study psychology, it was appropriate that he sought work in a psychiatric home as a nurse on a ward of 90 patients, some of whom had been First World War soldiers and had developed general paralysis of the insane as a result of contracting syphilis which had never been treated. Stan Rosenthal's decision to do this type of work had been influenced by two leading psychologists: Abe Maslow, Founder of the Humanistic Psychology Movement, and Vicktor Frankl who invented logo therapy. Much later Rosenthal was to contribute to the development of their theories when he wrote 'Self as Process' during his period of teaching at the Welsh College of Medicine.

There followed years of work as an interactive psychologist, beginning with a post with the Steel Company of Wales, then as a training officer in Education of Psychology. Subsequently he worked as a psychologist in the Market Research department of *The Sunday Times*. Later he was to enter academic life and then to take up the post of Welsh Office Senior Research Fellow. This may seem to have been a huge gap in a creative life. However, this was the context in which he developed his theory of creativity and art and also the philosophy which allowed him to become convinced of the value of process as opposed to the search for completeness. It enabled him to believe that in life and in the practice of art, the notion of 'moving on' should be central. This idea is also associated with the Zen concept of 'letting go' or learning not to try to grasp what is unattainable. In order to understand the steps which caused him to move on through the various gateways which were presented to him, it is important to unravel some of his fundamental ideas about art and creativity. Through his various written texts, Stan Rosenthal has examined both the motivation behind making art and also some aspects of the experience of mark-making. Through comparison with other human activities and an application of the scientific knowledge of physical and psychological responses occurring during certain experiences, he suggests a particular understanding of the nature of artistic practice. In one instance he deals with an idea that he calls 'intentionality'. He observes that:

> In order to discover what it is that the artist is or might be trying to achieve when engaged in the process of art, we need to consider what it is that he or she tries to express or record; we need to ask, does the artist work with the *intention* of externalising, of expressing, of producing a picture, a metaphor or a record, or could it be that these are only the by-products of what he or she is really, or intentionally, doing when engaged in the process of art.

The business of making works of art is therefore a complex process and one which can only be fully understood if it is possible to enter into the psychological focus of the maker. Another important issue that seems to relate closely to Stan Rosenthal's own practice as an artist is that of privilege and dialogue. He discusses this towards the end of his thesis, adapting the Zen concept to explain that:

> The world in which the individual artist works is a private world, the world of art, a world to which he or she is privy. It is a world, which, even without his or her conscious knowledge, the artist celebrates and commemorates through the very act of trying to access and understand; by entering into the intimate dialogue, without which there is no art.

. . . this dialogue, with its essential intimacy, with its nuances, proposals, arguments and counter-proposals has no means of retaining its intimacy; has no means by which it can avoid being or becoming its own external world record . . . the very nature of the dialogue itself, its self-recording, destroys the essential intimate privacy in which it is conducted. The work of visual art, the culmination of the process of art up to that instant, lays bare the conclusion of the dialogue, leaving it open to the scrutiny of those who look in order to see and understand.

GATEWAYS

All paths lead
to the gateless gate.
and here,
the rivers of enlightenment
become the boundless ocean
of eternity.

And if you seek to find
my contribution to mankind,
then you must journey
beyond the gateless gate,
and you will find it there,
a single drop of water.

Tekisui

In 1972 Stan Rosenthal published a small book, *Tao: the Gateless Gate*, which was a translation and interpretation of the writings of Taoist Philosophy. By 1984 he had also produced a translation and interpretation of *The Tao Te Ching by Lao Tzu*. These publications were a result of his deep involvement with Zen Buddhism and of his activities running a Zen group and teaching Tai Chi in Cardiff. By this time Stan had been a student of Zen Buddhism for twenty years. He had met D.T. Suzuki, a famous Zen teacher, in 1952 when he hitch-hiked from Leicester to hear a talk that Suzuki gave in London. Subsequently, he was to study under two other Zen teachers, one of whom taught through the military art of 'kendo'. By 1979, Stan Rosenthal was Welsh Office Senior Research Fellow in interactive psychology at the Welsh School of Medicine, having come to Wales in 1974 to take up a post with the South Glamorgan Area Health Authority. When this job came to an end, he went back to lecturing but soon decided that he wanted to leave this career altogether and to devote himself to Zen Buddhism. He fought successfully to get voluntary redundancy from his lecturing post and so became free to continue to teach Zen and Tai Chi. His relationship with his students became mutually supportive when Stan was persuaded to open a shop in which he sold bonsai trees and things made by the students.

During this period he was encouraged to have his eyes tested again and found that it would now be possible for him to take up art again. Thus for Stan Rosenthal to become an artist was to be the outcome of a series of entrances, an unfolding of life rather than a set course. Since the Zen philosophy had traditionally been written in Kanji, a pictographic language which is the basis of both Chinese and Japanese, and as its teaching frequently evokes images of simplicity and symbolic meaning, it was no surprise that Stan Rosenthal soon began to paint in a Zen-influenced way. He also learned the various calligraphic styles in order to illustrate his books on Zen philosophy.

The first Zen painting that Stan Rosenthal produced was a version of an old scroll-painting that belonged to one of his students. The simple brush image of the silhouettes of three men watching the moon is visually linked to the circular form by the vertical lines of Running Script, which seem to dance on the page. They create the following haiku text:

> Composing Haiku
> Sitting in the Great Guest Hall
> The moon advancing.

COMPOSING HAIKU

To an untaught eye, the form of the Running Script, which is the essence of the art of Zen painting, often seems to suggest the form of a dancing figure, executing strong arabesques and smoothly linked shapes. However, the flow of the line is fundamental to this type of work and in Hitzuzandu Painting it is considered that the picture is made the instant that the pen first touches the paper. 'One Instant of Great Joy' is an example of this,

LAUGHTER AND TEARS   ONE INSTANT OF GREAT JOY

as is also the entirely calligraphic work, 'Between Heaven and Earth, laughter and tears, laughter and tears'. Other paintings have a more Chinese character and carry thoughtful messages from the Tao Te Ching. Perhaps the most beautiful of Rosenthal's Zen paintings to Western eyes would be those in which he has used an older style of writing for which the artist used a hollowed bamboo shoot, fibre cord and ink. The image is soft, faintly bleeding at the edges of the marks and has a rich, black intensity similar to that achieved in lithography.

Although the Zen paintings were exhibited at the time and he had a successful exhibition and residency at the Plymouth Theatre Royal, they have not been seen in public in recent years. The landscape painting, which is the core of his work, has derived from a different source of inspiration. But there are connections between these two strands of his work, and some of the typical images of his Buddhist work reappear in the Pembrokeshire paintings. The most obvious of these is the circular form, read as the sun or the moon, which both types of work share. It is to be found in many compositions, such as 'Carreg Samson and Strumble Head' and 'Pembrokeshire Coast Path' and in the almost abstract prints, 'St. David's Head' and 'Green Lane Tretio', both shown overleaf. The recent paintings are also characterised by a tendency to simplify landscape forms and to introduce strong linear elements, which may derive from the Running Script calligraphic style of his earlier work.

St David's Head   Green Lane, tretio

There may be a more significant influence of the Zen period on his current career as an artist, in that Stan Rosenthal produces several versions of the same image or theme and also reproduces work in a variety of media. The way in which certain subjects have inspired him to produce several different works is amply illustrated in this book by the section entitled, appropiately, 'Returning'. This way of working is connected to the idea that the actual object that is the subject of the painting is itself a part of the process of making a work of art. As well as allowing more people to own a particular image, this confirms his belief that everything is process. No one impression of a seen image is the absolute, as everything in nature is transitory, affected as it is by constant change in climatic and other conditions. Thus the artist's interpretation of a thing is inevitably different from the thing that has been used as the starting point for the image.

Know that you are not the centre of the universe and that all things are subject to change. Accept transience, the inevitable and the irrevocable. Seek liberation from self delusion and deceit, from hatred, envy, greed and rage. Learn to let go of that which cannot be held, or is destroyed by grasping. By these means you will obviate much suffering.

Carreg Samson is one of the places to which the artist has been drawn on many occasions. It is a cromlech built in the megalithic period as a burial chamber. Now without its original covering of earth, it is a circle of huge upright rough stones, standing tightly together in order to support the immense capstone. The whole resembles a giant and misshapen toadstool. One version of the image focuses on the unwieldy form itself, investing the rocks with a dynamic quality through the lively brushwork and the touches of flame and white on their surfaces. Another depicts the cromlech dwarfed by the stretched form of Pen-caer reaching out to sea as Strumble Head. The black outlines of clouds, which swirl above the peninsula and crowd the red, setting sun, also reflect the shape of the famous capstone and effectively make it seem more elemental in character. The artist recalls one particular occasion on which he saw the stones.

CARREG SAMSON AND STRUMBLE HEAD

The night sky was clear, but there was a mist hovering about one metre above the ground. We took a detour to see Carreg Samson (I had already painted it twice), and it was magical, with the mist floating about around the standing stones that support the capstone. I must admit that much of the picture, which I started work on next day, is from my imagination, but I believe that this particular picture comes closest to the neo-Romantic tradition.

A PRIVILEGED PLACE

For some people the name Grongar Hill will evoke a series of connected memories, all related to the notion that individual landscapes evoke a special emotion and are endowed with unusual qualities. This idea may originate in the influence of a particular work of art, music or literature rather than in the real physical characteristics of the place itself. Its influence is created by the sifting and defining power of the creative imagination. Grongar Hill is a small, rounded area of upland in Carmarthenshire, which today appears unremarkable, dotted as it is with white farmhouses, with grazing sheep, clumps of trees and irregular field boundaries. However, in a poem written in 1726, John Dyer invested the place with an idyllic quality. He wrote as a devotee of the fashionable love of a pastoral and lyrical landscape and from the affection that he had for a place very close to his home.

Ever charming, ever new,
When will the landskip tire the view.
The fountain's fall, the river's flow,
The woody vallies warm and low,
The windy summit wild and high,
Roughly rushing on the sky.

The pleasant seat, the ruin'd tow'r,

The naked rock, the shady bow'r,

The town and village, dome and farm,

Each give each a double charm,

As pearls upon an Eithiop's arm.

John Dyer 1726

Dyer's poem and the admiration that it caused for a landscape that is both rugged and yet intimate was an important influence on the neo-Romantic tradition in painting. After the Second World War and its threats to the traditional British landscape there was a great nostalgia for rural life as it had been and for a certain type of landscape. Dyer's influence, combined with the remoteness and ancient history associated with parts of west Wales, brought a number of artists to the area. Perhaps on the way to Pembrokeshire, Grongar Hill offered itself as a place to stop and contemplate the idea of an ideal landscape and, to artists, it offered a marvellous subject for painting. From the late 1930s, John Piper made several very different paintings interpreting this landscape and Stan Rosenthal explains that he was impressed by one that he saw in 1947. He did not then know where Grongar Hill was, but carried the image with him in his mind for the next fifty years.

In some way it was this interest in the neo-Romantics and in Grongar Hill which finally brought him to Pembrokeshire and set him on the course of becoming a landscape painter. Subsequently he has painted his own versions of this theme in which the rounded shapes are exaggerated to a greater sensuality. In one instance, a ghostly blue light from the moon loses detail but suggests a restless, heaving of the undulating land.

It was Pembrokeshire itself, however, which was to entrap Stan Rosenthal's imagination and 'Summer Storm on the Cleddau' was the first painting that he made of a Pembrokeshire subject, marking his decision to live in that part of Wales. He describes how he and his wife, Nicola, had driven to the area on business.

We finished early, and went to Picton Ferry, where Graham Sutherland used to paint. It was a still, golden evening and I started painting. The sky began to darken in the south, and great drops of rain began to fall into the river, like silver melting into gold. We dashed for the car, and drove home soaking wet. Before we arrived back in Cardiff we had decided to move to Pembrokeshire.

It is rarely easy to change one's personal and professional life at the same time and the decision to move to a new place adds to the challenge. This is what happened to Stan Rosenthal at the age of 55. He had met Nicola when he joined a life-drawing class in

Cardiff, run by his friend, the ceramic sculptor Mike Flynn. Their relationship caused them both to rethink their lives. Nicola chose not to go to Art College but to join Stan and to set up a business. Their first attempts to do this in South Pembrokeshire did not work well and so they soon moved to St Davids, where Stan had a studio and Nicola opened a craft shop next door. Gradually the craft business was replaced by a gallery for the sale of Stan's work and that of other local artists. From then Stan's work became increasingly popular, especially when he began to produce limited-edition prints and reproductions of his work. Eventually they were given the chance to move to Mabws Fawr, a previous farm complex, and in 2001 opened a studio gallery there. Together with the opportunity to begin to produce his own prints through the purchase of printing equipment, this has opened yet another gateway for the artist, which has been especially supported by Nicola's collaboration.

During the years spent in Pembrokeshire Stan Rosenthal's ideas about the nature of landscape painting have taken shape and developed. He has come to believe that the

SUMMER STORM ON THE CLEDDAU

landscape artist is especially privileged because of the way in which he or she experiences landscape. Art critic Hugh de Loy makes precisely this point:

> The landscape painter occupies a privileged place in society, spending his working life communing with nature in all its vagaries, observing at first hand the changing of the light, the seasons, and prevailing climatic conditions, all of which come together in what Stan Rosenthal describes as 'the miracle of art', and what most of us think of as inspiration.
>
> As though to further engage the artist in this dialogue, and almost jealously, as though to retain his undivided attention, nature seems to be able, when she is willing, to provide a spectacle of rare and transient beauty, so localized that it seems to be directed to only the one individual, as though she is flirting, or sharing an intimate secret with a lover or a very close friend.

The idea that an artist has a special relationship with nature, even a deep empathy, was at the heart of much of nineteenth-century romanticism and this belief is resurrected by the neo-Romantics. Stan Rosenthal illustrates the privilege that he feels in his description of his experience of the 'red flash', an experience that he has taken several times as the inspiration for original paintings. The 'red flash' is a rare phenomenon which occurs on a few occasions a year at isolated spots on the Pembrokeshire coast and which is actually caused by the high level of infra-red saturation in the light around the north Pembrokeshire coast. Stan Rosenthal describes the intensity of the experience which he has had on each of the three occasions when he has seen the 'red flash'.

> During these fleeting occurrences, which occur invariably only at sunrise or sunset, over a distance of a few hundred yards, everything within that space upon which light is cast, including the very air itself, appears to be suddenly bathed in a deep red glow, so strong that to the unknowing observer, it is quite awesome. When it first appears, it seems to burst with an intensity of light said by some to be 'as blinding as the blackness of the night'. It then disappears as suddenly as it appeared. But those who have witnessed it describe the instant for which it exists as a journey into the sublime.

The paintings which transcribe this experience are characterised by a dominating foreground of intense red behind which floats the subdued twilight shadows of headlands and sea. They are near to the feeling for the absolute value and power of saturated colour which was exploited by abstract expressionist artists – such as Mark Rothko in his famous paintings from the 1950s. However, Stan Rosenthal is intent on keeping in touch with the original source of his image and of using the image that he makes as a vehicle by which his audience can also enter into his privileged experience. For him the painting or print is a part of that process by which a special personal way of seeing is redefined by its reproduction as an image and then becomes open to a further process of change and interpretation through the way that it is experienced or used by other people. He explains that the original motif, 'an external world object', becomes a 'new external world object' in the form of the picture as a real object.

The Silent Sentinels of Dewisland

Many of Stan Rosenthal's paintings can be described as dealing with discovery and revelation and with a landscape which is full of almost hidden detail, where the minutiae are important. This is an aspect of the Pembrokeshire landscape which has frequently been commented upon and is certainly one which has made it attractive to certain artists. Sutherland's early work in Pembrokeshire focused on the narrow lanes and standing stones, concrete evidence of human activity, while his later work identified individual trees, roots and rocks and gave them metaphorical meaning by suggesting human feeling and comparisons with images such as the Crucifixion. John Piper, on the other hand, was less swayed by the mystical aspects of the landscape and was more intent to focus on the presence of the specific textures, the familiar outlines of rocky outcrops and the ragged shapes of ruined buildings. 'Garn Fawr 1979' is a particularly subtle and atmospheric example of Piper's later work in Pembrokeshire. Rosenthal's relationship with this landscape is probably closer to that of John Piper. He explains that he is not interested in fabricated Victorian Celticism but he loves the resonance of pre-Celtic history, which is present all around him. In response to this he feels drawn to the small, coastal outcrops of the St Davids peninsula and perceives them to be watching as silent sentinels over this mysterious and ancient landscape.

The painting 'Dewisland Skyline' is a watercolour in which the craggy line of hills is seen from a distance and beneath a huge, watery sky. Usually Rosenthal focuses his care on an individual hillscape. Carn Llidi is one of the 'silent sentinels of Dewisland', which has most frequently appeared in his work. The version entitled 'Poppies at Carn Llidi' shows the knobbly hill, once an island but now beached on the edge of the land. It is framed by an aurora of gold, which is held in place by dark clouds, themselves mimicking the shapes of the rock. Pen-caer is another place which the artist depicts as a watchful guardian of the land. Indeed, as its name indicates, this was one of many places on this coast where there were ancient hill forts, looking anxiously out to sea. Garn Fawr (the Big Cairn) is the knob in the middle of this piece of land and is seen thrusting into a red sky in a number of his

13

images. Stan Rosenthal has also been attracted to other places which have a similar character: forts on crags, such as Carreg Cennen in Carmarthenshire; Cadair Idris, the great guardian mountain at the south of Snowdonia. He obviously senses the huge force that has made such rocks and mountains rise up out of a volcanic sea and which have created the special western landscape. In 'Cadair Idris, Easter 2001' he has simplified the massive shape of Mynydd Moel rising above Llyn Cau, giving his vision of the folding and squeezing which pushed the mountain into being so long ago.

In some respects the process of buckling and forcing the land into shape is exaggerated in the series of Serigraphs depicting small settlements on the Pembrokeshire coast. These are Porthclais, Felinganol, Melin Trefin and Garn Fawr. He explains their inter-relation:

> I chose these specific locations to produce as a set of four, because they each encapsulate the little hills and valleys that form the coastline of the county. Each of these places has some special feature…Melin Trefin is the subject of one of the favourite poems in the Welsh language, describing the old (corn) mill which hasn't ground corn for many years. The standing stones on top of the hill look quite magical, as does the path down to the sea past the ruin of the mill building on the right of the picture.

FELINGANOL

Each painting in this series reveals the sensual aspect of the landscape, emphasising the femininity of its rolling forms and the protective way in which tiny buildings are tucked into folds or perched beside steep, curving lanes. The non-naturalistic combination of red, purple, yellow and green for all this series suggests warmth and opulence, a transformation of the hard landscape into a more exotic place. Other images which demonstrate a similar attention to detail and love of the most intimate of landscapes are those based on Mabws Fawr, where the artist now lives. In this instance the overwhelming colour is green, textured by the tiny stylised shapes of trees and flowers. The house itself is barely seen, lost among this sumptuous, fertile landscape, but beckoning as if in a fairy story.

Paintings Become Objects

The visitor arrives at Mabws Fawr, where the artist and his wife now live, perhaps casually drawn along the lane by the sign announcing the presence of the gallery or perhaps coming because he or she has at last tracked the artist down, having first spotted his work on the internet. There is a cluster of buildings of which one is Stan and Nicola Rosenthal's home, studio and gallery. The entrance is welcoming, flanked by plants, collected objects and the bric-a-brac of a country garden. It leads into a vestibule where Stan's work is displayed in the form of greeting cards and small prints. It may be tempting to browse here and some visitors will return home only with a carefully chosen card as a reminder of Pembrokeshire and of the colourful creativity of Stan Rosenthal. However, for others, the temptation to enter into the artist's imagination is overwhelming, the lure of the selection of pictures on show will be too great, and they will choose at least a print or maybe, an original painting.

The gallery is crowded with objects, things that have been collected over the years, mirrors, cabinets and carved objects. There is ample testimony to the love of texture and materials that the artist and his wife enjoy. To wander around is to be tempted to touch the rough carved wood of a piece of folk art or the smoother surface of tiles and ceramics. Amongst the collected objects are things that are reminiscent of Stan Rosenthal's own paintings, but it may take a few minutes to recognise them and to realise that they are alternative versions of his own work. The dynamic of process has again taken hold and his paintings are transformed and made to enter a different 'external world' through the skills of another craftsperson. There are embroideries, ceramics, stained glass, stone carving and fabrics. They invite us to ask why have they been made and to ponder on why an artist should want to reproduce, interpret, change, something created by another. Who has taken the trouble to carefully craft these things?

Rachel Wait and Richard Tong run 'Cardiff Embroidery Co.', in which they use digital technology to produce designs for a wide variety of clients who want embroidered motifs on clothing or other products. The images are then machine-embroidered. They usually work on designs which are relatively easy to adapt to the processes used, as the computer has to work out the number, density and direction of the stitches necessary to

EMBROIDERY

achieve the required effect. Rachel first saw Stan Rosenthal's paintings when she went for a weekend holiday near Whitesands Bay and she responded to his paintings by suggesting that they would look very good as embroideries. Having made this suggestion to the artist, she was pleased when he explained that he had himself thought of doing this, but did not know of anyone who could carry the idea through. It seemed to be a recipe for collaboration and so Rachel returned to Cardiff with some illustrations of Stan's work. It proved to be a quite demanding task to convert the images into a digitised form because the density of the colour that is used in the paintings required additional cross-stitches to be added in to the design. 'Poppy Cottage', one of the first designs they developed, required over 4,500 stitches and took about an hour and a quarter to produce on the embroidery machine. Successful work on several other images, such as 'Pistyll Rhaeadr' and 'Porth-gain', followed and it is likely that Cardiff Embroidery Co. will continue to make between four and six embroidered versions of selected examples of Stan Rosenthal's work.

Ceramicist Mark Walford has only lived in Pembrokeshire since 1999 but soon met Stan and Nicola Rosenthal and began to sell his crystal glaze ceramics in their shop in St Davids. He tells the story that one day he showed Stan a sculptural piece of work based on fleshy leaf forms reminiscent of the art nouveau style and inspired by a trip to Barcelona, where he had seen this exuberant decoration. The ceramic appealed to Stan and he immediately saw the possibility of developing this design, asking Mark if he could make a larger, vase-like piece, which would be coloured in the style of his own paintings. After

THE STILE

CERAMIC BY MARK WALFORD

Mark had made this they then looked at a slab pot which Stan owned and which suggested another idea, that of making slab ceramic versions of some of Stan's paintings. Mark Walford explains that the chunky, colourful, simplified style and forms of the paintings lend themselves to reproduction in slab form, and as he progressed with the work on the initial ten pieces, he found that the painted images were beginning to influence his own creative approach. He became freer in his interpretation of the paintings, the ceramics gaining their own existence and even combining several different images, which blend into one as they encircle the pot. Eventually Mark Walford began to make some individual pots which were to his own design but which portrayed similar views of the Preseli hills, the Gwaun Valley and of Pentre Ifan cromlech. The relationship has been a profitable one for both artists on several levels and Mark enthusiastically reflects that '. . . knowing Stan has enriched my life.'

This idea is reiterated by Chris Tancock, who has made stone carvings related to Stan Rosenthal's work. Chris Tancock suggests that Stan does tend to influence other artists, who find that they can use his work as a stepping-off point for their own creativity. His own experience of this began with a commission to make a piece based on one of Stan's works. He then went on to make about twelve other carvings that were related to the paintings. These were shell-like sculptures, based on eroded elements, rather like paths that curve through landscape shapes. Chris Tancock's own work has a basis in design and he is currently most interested in photography. However, even in this work there are some reminiscences of his relationship with Stan Rosenthal as he manipulates prints to bring together panoramic aspects of a place and create a composite image. Again, the process is fundamental to the work and there is no preconceived 'product'.

SCULPTURE BY CHRIS TANCOCK

'SEEK NEITHER BRILLIANCE NOR THE VOID'

Stan Rosenthal's work is collected by a great number of people, but he does not consider himself to be a 'famous artist', nor is he particularly concerned with critical acclaim. He is happy to show work in places that are not galleries because that enables people who would not normally go to a gallery to see the work: he has even hung work in a McDonald's cafe and in a Wimpy bar. However, his paintings are also exhibited in prestigious venues. He has been exhibited in the Pentigili project for the National Eisteddfod of Wales, in the National Assembly of Wales building and at St David's Hall, in the Cardiff 'Summer Exhibition'.

It has been said that people in Britain are less likely to buy prints than the public in most European countries. However, the success of Stan's work in this form tends to disprove this notion and his work has become very popular, often with people who would not usually be able to afford a work of art. Tourists often come to the gallery as casual visitors and leave with a print. There is now an astonishingly large network of people who own his work and this gives him the satisfaction that so many others are entering into the 'privilege' of his way of seeing the Pembrokeshire landscape. He is pleased that a number of schools in Britain and some in Europe use examples of his work in teaching students ways of seeing and describing and of learning what he would describe as 'the miracle of art'.

Most collectors of Stan Rosenthal's work make a personal visit to his studio and may travel a long way. These visits often result in commissions, for which the artist produces an original work. A few collectors each now own more pieces of Stan Rosenthal's work than does the artist himself. However many works a collector owns, the artist is always interested to learn why they have chosen those particular images and in what way they contribute to their enjoyment of visual experience.

It is particularly heartening for the artist when local people are able to delight in his work. A local collector, TS, who called in at Stan's Pembrokeshire gallery very regularly, is particularly appreciative of how the artist's subjects may remain consistent over the years, but his perspectives and approaches change and develop.

SEEK NEITHER BRILLIANCE NOR THE VOID

'What I like about Stan's work in particular is the fact that it is ever changing. I mean this in two ways: firstly that when you see one of his pictures in a different light the picture itself seems to have changed; and secondly that he does not stay still in his search for his 'ideal picture'. He continues to experiment, maybe visiting and revisiting the same view on a number of occasions, each time producing an image quite different from its predecessor. This is why it is so exciting for me to visit his studio and gallery, which is easier for me than it is for most of his friends and collectors, because we live only a few miles away.'

Some collectors are aware that the pleasure they derive from the work is linked to spiritual sustenance. This is aptly explained by the Reverend Michael Robinson, vicar of St Peter's, Hale.

'Stan's works are well worth looking at for those who are interested in genuine spirituality . . . Contemplation is not only the preserve of the saint. It is open to anyone with eyes to see what an inspired piece of art has to tell us about the real meaning of life.'

In discussing the personal impact of an artist's work on collectors and critics, it is often the effect of one particular work with which we identify the artist's whole achievement. One painting may stay in the memory and provide recurring stimulation and pleasure. Erica Smith describes (in catalogue notes, 1988) what it is that moves her in one particular painting by Stan of the Brecon Beacons:

'In the foreground, golden grasses seem to wave in the breeze. The horizon is low, probably only a quarter of the height in the picture. Above it is golden space. In the top right-hand corner soars a tiny bird, a Red Kite, seeming to delight in its freedom. The title of this picture is appropriate; not only to this picture, but also to the Zen philosophy he has brought with him to his art. It is called, 'And then I saw the Red Kite rising.'

There is a great value, therefore, in actually possessing a work of art that has the effect that Erica Smith has expressed. It is possible to return to it daily and renew the experience. Mike Parker writes the *The Rough Guide to Wales*. He spends a lot of his time wandering the country, checking out accommodation, tourist venues, what things cost, where best to go and what to avoid. It isn't at all glamorous and sometimes it's a hard slog. There are occasions, though, when a bit of bright light illuminates a place and gets him really involved. He looks up from his computer and the endless stream of words, glances at his pictures, framed glowing on the walls of his house, and remembers Pembrokeshire and his visit to Stan Rosenthal's studio. He has become a part of the process in which the beached rocks of south-west Wales, the coast, the white cottages and the standing stones make their presence now in the slated village where he lives. This is what paintings can do: they take one place to another; they have memories; they are containers of memory.

SHELAGH HOURAHANE

DISCOVERIES

AND

REVELATIONS

GRONGAR HILL

Although this picture is quite recent, I have put it first because it is one of my favourites, and because it has a history that dates back to my time in art college, over fifty years ago.

Early in 1947 my family moved from Luton to Southend-on-Sea in Essex. Shortly before my 14th birthday in April of that year I was accepted at the local college to study art. As I remember it now, we had a number of visits from well-known artists, one being Graham Sutherland, and another was John Piper. Before they came to visit, I found books about them so I would be familiar with their work, and could ask them questions. When the time came, though, I did not speak to them. I found Sutherland to be somewhat cool (in seeming contradiction to his work, which seemed to me to be very warm and intimate). One book I had found was a volume illustrated by John Piper entitled *English, Scottish and Welsh Landscape*, edited by John Betjeman and Geoffrey Taylor. It contained a number of original lithographs by John Piper, one of which was called 'Grongar Hill'. It illustrated an extract from the poem of the same name, written by John Dyer who lived in the first half of the 18th century.

Prior to this time I did not know the work of John Piper, but I fell in love with his illustrations in the book, all of which were printed with a limited range of colours, seemingly grey, black and yellow. I was particularly drawn to his image of Grongar Hill, even though I knew nothing about the poem, nor of the area where the hill is situated.

I meant to ask John Piper questions about his illustrations and the location of the place, but it I was too nervous to do so. This was mainly because of his height, and my shyness at that age (I was still only fourteen at the time). Nevertheless, I determined then that one day I would draw this strange, mysterious place. Bearing in mind that in 1947 very few people had cars, and there were no motorways, travel was not as frequently undertaken as it is today. I remember looking through various books and at railway travel posters to find the whereabouts of Carmarthenshire, and when I discovered it was in Wales, it seemed a million miles away from Essex where we lived at the time.

Eventually the family moved to Leicester and by the time I was seventeen, I was hitch-hiking around the country, usually at night, so that I could draw at my point of arrival the following day. I did get to north Wales, but as a young man I never made it to south-west Wales to discover the whereabouts of Grongar Hill.

Half a century later, after living in a variety of places, and having met Nicola, I was living and working in Pembrokeshire. By chance, whilst looking through a printer's sample book in our collection, I found a copy of the poem and a small copy of the illustration. In

the meantime, we had also discovered another reference to Grongar Hill in *Under Milk Wood* by Dylan Thomas, in the Reverend Eli Jenkins's prayer.

Soon after, Nicola and I set off for Carmarthen to look for Grongar Hill. We called in at the museum as we passed by, where the staff pointed us in the right direction, marking the hill on a map we had with us.

After losing our way a couple of times we saw what we thought must be Grongar Hill, but we were on the road just below the hill, and too close to see it clearly. So we climbed up the hill on the other side of the road, to Llangethan church. In the churchyard, we found the spot where John Piper must have stood over half a century before. I then drew a sketch of the hill from the same viewpoint, and when we left the church, I turned round and drew it from the road.

This was not to be the end of the story, though, because some time later I happened to tell a good friend of ours, Hugh Fowler-Wright, about my fifty-year search. A few days later, to our great delight, there appeared in the post a copy of the very book where I had first seen a picture of the hill, a gift from Hugh that was very much appreciated.

A little while later we were able to purchase a copy of the poem, published with notes by the John Hopkins University Press in 1941. Its significance in literary circles is due to the fact that it is believed to be the first, or one of the first, landscape poems in the English language. The frontispiece to the book shows John Dyer reclining under a black Thorn Tree on Grongar Hill, looking at his home, Aberglasne, with Dryslwyn Castle in the background.

Using my sketch of Grongar Hill, I eventually painted an image of it as though lit by moonlight. When we obtained our own printing equipment I reworked the image, and it has proved to be very popular.

As though to bring a this fifty-year adventure to a close, a little while later we heard from another friend, Mike Goldmark, that another lithograph by John Piper had become available, showing the hill from a different viewpoint. Nicola purchased it for my birthday, and it now hangs in our sitting room.

Llangattam

25

WILLOW

This image was started about forty years ago. I had been looking at some rimpa paintings (pictures painted on a gold background) in a book on Japanese art, and decided I wanted to paint one myself. At the time I had just started a family, and we very short of money, living in two rooms of a tiny terraced house in Porthcawl. I was hardly painting at all during that period, but decided I would attempt a rimpa painting.

I found a canvas board with a picture I did not like, so I scrubbed it down and painted over it. I then applied mixes of gold and various colours, at first using a brush, and then a roller. After many applications, I was happy with the background, but the actual design of the image (to paint onto the 'field') presented a problem because I could not decide what image to use. After a couple of months, I gave up, wrapped the picture to protect it, and put it under the bed.

Many house-moves later, living in Cardiff, I found the somewhat tattered parcel, and was surprised to discover the surface was still undamaged. Remembering the decision-making problem I had encountered previously, I thought about it no more for over a year. Then, a 'thank you' postcard I received from an Australian hitch-hiker I had picked up gave me an idea.

Without thinking about it any further, I painted the willow fronds. Fortunately, they turned out well, because had they not done so, I could not have removed them without damaging the remaining surface.

The 'chop' (the red seal, bottom left) is a name I was given by one of my Zen teachers. It is 'Kotan', which means 'elegant simplicity', with the symbols in the border representing the senses.

The signature above the chop is my actual Zen name, 'ishida' in Japanese, and 'Shi-tien' in Mandarin Chinese. In both languages it means 'stony field', which is the meaning of the name Stanley.

LEET AT TAVISTOCK

(WITH SLUICE GATE CLOSED, AND WITH SLUICE GATE OPEN)

Immediately after a period as artist in residence at Plymouth Theatre Royal, I went to stay with some friends at Tavistock. They lived in an old converted mill near the river, with a leet running close to the house. Although the mill was long gone, as I remember, the leet was opened from time to time to help release some water from the river when it was running high. For the most part, though, it was very shallow, with quite a sandy bottom that could be clearly seen.

Whilst staying there I tried to draw a picture of the water running, but failed miserably on the first couple of days. Then I started a picture using coloured pencils, with a little more success. I took some photographs to provide me with a 'frozen instant', but intended to start a painting the next day.

The following day, after breakfast, I went to the leet, but it was completely different because the sluice had been opened, and the water was high, rushing by, and quite

turbulent. Although I could 'see' it would make a very impressive image, I was unprepared for what I saw, and could not adjust to it. I took more photographs, with the intention of painting it later during my stay (in a caravan in the garden).

Unfortunately I had caught a chest infection, and my daughter Judith provided an excuse for me to return home, and I did so. (If I had not done so, I might never have met Nicola, but that is another story). I had the photographs developed a few days later, and painted the two images a short time after that.

They were both painted in oils, partly with a brush, and partly by pallet knife, on gold printed (sized) Fabbriano paper, and marked my change from painting in the 'zen tradition' of the willow painting shown previously, to a more European, somewhat impressionist style. For that reason, and because they were painted at the time I met Nicola, we have kept them for our own collection.

I like the two images as a pair because they show the differences that can be seen by returning to a place previously visited.

COEDMOR FROM RHOSHILL

The right-hand wing of the mansion house, Coedmor, was our home for a short time whilst I was the artist in residence there, for the owner, Peregrine (Pel) Rayner. We have retained our friendship with Pel since we met on a visit nearby to pick up a stick chair, and have watched four of his children grow up into fine young men and women.

The house stands on the Teifi gorge, and is in Ceredigion, although the picture was painted looking across the field of the river valley from Rhoshill, and therefore depicts a Pembrokeshire landscape. The house is one of the most historic in west Wales, having a connection to the Welsh Prince Llywelyn.

Cilgerran Castle is virtually opposite, and one morning I sat on a window seat in the music room to draw the castle. Pel told me how the painter Turner had painted the castle from the same spot; after that I could never finish the picture . . . perhaps I will one day.

When I painted Coedmor from Rhoshill, the field in the foreground was not ploughed, but I decided to paint it as though it were, in order to use the ploughed lines to increase the feeling of depth through the perspective, and to 'take the viewer's eye' to the house. Interestingly, it was later ploughed, and in the same direction as I had imagined it. I was unaware of the religious symbolism of ploughed fields at the time, but I was told of it later, by a friend who is a vicar. I painted the plough-lines by scratching out colour and then over-painting in another shade to give texture.

Anyone who has read my theory of art (summarised for inclusion in this book) will know I that I believe the true subject mater of a picture is sometimes other than what it appears to be (or even what it is known as), and in this instance it could be that the popularity of the image is due to the symbolism of the ploughed field, and that it is this part of the image that is its 'quintessential aesthetic'.

AS I AWOKE

This image shows the gable end of the old captain's cottage where Nicola and I lived in north Pembrokeshire. There could hardly have been a greater contrast between two homes then there was between Coedmor mansion and the house in Solva. Although I had produced large collage and montage work whilst at art college, this was the first return to the idea of composing a picture from composite elements. There was a large apple tree in that garden, and during the late summer, as the apples ripened, they would fall onto the roof of the house, immediately above the bedroom. Until we discovered what it was that caused the noise, it was quite disconcerting.

We had very good neighbours in Solva, which is probably why we enjoyed our time there so much. Solva is a very pretty village but apart from its natural beauty, the people who live there are very pleasant in their manner. Many of the older villagers are the descendants of sailors who worked aboard the square riggers and schooners which plied their trade out of a little harbour at the foot of the hill. There are still a number of menfolk in the village who earn their livelihood from fishing.

The light strip (top left in the picture) represents the effect of the pupils of my eyes not reacting quickly enough to the bright, early-morning sun, bleaching out the colour as I threw open the curtains too quickly . . . not to be recommended.

PORTH-GAIN

It is well known amongst my friends and acquaintances that I have a childlike fascination for working boats, fishermen and other seafarers, as well as for the little ports and harbours which are their havens. Porth-gain is one of those havens, which, like Solva, is on the north Pembrokeshire coast.

The old ruins of the industrial past loom above the harbour where local fishermen still regularly put out to seek to earn their living. One of them is Rob, a fisherman whom I am proud to call a friend (and to whom I'm eternally grateful for single-handedly beating my inglenook fireplace back into shape with an enormous sledge-hammer when he helped to renovate Plas y Mabws, where we lived for some years).

The quarries close to Porth-gain were a source of slate and dolerite, used for road-making, at the end of the 19th century and the early part of the 20th century. These natural resources were shipped out of Porth-gain, but the tiny harbour was so small that the boats could not sail into the harbour on their own power, and had to be winched in by a method known as 'warping'.

I think my sentiments concerning Porth-gain are communicated well in this image. The bright colours and simplified shapes with their strong black outlines still make me smile when I look at the painting. Though it is not obvious, this image was in fact composed from three sketches, each drawn from a different viewpoint, and then pulled together to compress the width of the image.

SANDY HAVEN

Sandy Haven is one of those places which serves as a link between Graham Sutherland and myself. Like many others, we discovered it when we were tracing his footsteps (and those of John Piper) in Pembrokeshire. It hardly needs to be said that I was delighted when Hugh de Loy suggested that I might be considered 'their worthy successor, taking off from where they stopped.' (He made this generous comment at the opening of the Pembrokeshire studio to the public in 2001.)

Apparently, many years ago, Graham and Kathleen Sutherland sought accommodation at the house in the foreground, but were turned away because the landlady thought they might be spies. We were told this by the landlady's daughter, some sixty or more years later. Graham and Kathleen were always very well dressed, and from the description we received it was easy to imagine them standing in their London attire at the door of the cottage by a tiny creek on the Milford Haven waterway. It was probably even more incongruous because, as Graham himself was to later describe it in a letter to a friend, he and Kathleen had arrived at Sandy Haven only because he had got lost on the narrow winding lanes of Pembrokeshire.

The picture is painted in watercolour, pen and ink, a technique widely used earlier this century for book illustration.

PORTHCLAIS

The little inlets and the valleys leading down to the sea around the coast of Pembrokeshire are especially fascinating for me. It may seem strange to someone living in a rural area, but the little ports and quays remind me of the tiny docks on the Thames where I lived as a child. Although the docklands area was full of warehouses and depositories, to a child, the streets were canyons, and the tall buildings were cliffs, casting gigantic shadows across Lower Thames Street and Puddle Dock. Where the Thames sailing barges would put down, their flat bottoms settling on the grid iron platforms built for that purpose alongside the quays.

I was told by a Pembrokeshire fisherman that the red-ochre-sailed vessels that I watched as a child also sailed to places such as Porthclais, the little harbour I have painted a number of times in various media and styles. On this occasion I chose to formalize the shapes in order to accentuate them. Graham Sutherland painted a semi-abstract picture of Porthclais from a nearby viewpoint, and I have taken a number of classes there when working as visiting lecturer to his collection. It is quite a magic spot; once a very busy harbour, it is said to be the place where the wild boar from the Mabinogion came ashore. It is also where the purple sandstone for Saint Davids Cathedral was landed, having been sailed round from Carn Nwchwn.

RED PEMBROKESHIRE COTTAGE

This tiny cottage is at the side of the road between Haverfordwest and Dale. It is very typical of many such cottages to be seen in the rural areas of west Wales, and known as 'Tai Unnos' – literally, One-night Homes. These were dwellings built on common land, which, if they were started one day and had smoke coming out of the chimney by the next morning, were deemed in common law to be rightfully owned by the builder. A group of friends might work together to complete one, and then start another nearby. The boundaries were determined by throwing an axe a number of times from the cottage, the places where the axe landed forming the boundary.

Although there are many white and pink-coloured cottages today, during the eighteenth and nineteenth centuries they were commonly painted deep red, with a wash made from mixing lime with bull's blood (and sometimes dung). These cottages would often consist of only one room, or two if the building was big enough to be divided down the middle by a partition screen. The two rooms would serve as a living room (and bedroom for the mother and father) and a bedroom for the children. The adults would frequently sleep in a box bed close by the *simne fawr* (inglenook).

It was not uncommon for a tiny cottage such as this to be home to a family of five or six in the last century and the early 1900s. A few years ago this ancient right was formalized under the Registration of Land Act.

There are very few of them left today, but many were later enlarged, while some were demolished and a house built on the site. One such property came to my attention when it was to be sold a few years ago. It had been held in the same family for over one hundred years, and it took quite a long time to sort out the ownership because it had never been registered.

POPPY COTTAGE

The tiny hamlet of Maes y Mynydd is situated north of Treleddyd Fawr, near Saint Davids. It was once a Quaker (Society of Friends) settlement, and the village was known as Pennsylvania at that time. It is linked to Treleddyd Fawr by a green lane. For a period of about forty years during the 19th century, the green lane was known as The Road to New York, and Maes y Mynydd was called Pennsylvania because the inhabitants hoped to emigrate there.

Maes y Mynydd now consists of about twelve ruined buildings, and what was once the lane through the group of houses is now overgrown, but it is a mass of wild flowers in the spring and summer months. It appears that some of the buildings were thatched, but were then grouted over to prevent the thatch from lifting in the strong winds which prevail in the coastal areas during the winter. These grouted roofs were not uncommon in north Pembrokeshire, and they covered slate as well as thatch.

The northern coastal plain, where Poppy Cottage is situated, is open to the northerly winds, and it is probably for this reason that other people did not build there. It is also probable that the people who did choose to build there did so because of its isolation (because they were not welcomed in the area). During that period there was considerable antagonism between the chapels and churches. And there are some elderly people still living in the area who barely even speak to their neighbours because, as children, they were told not to do so if they attended a different chapel or church.

WATERCOLOURS

These three images were painted within a few months of each other. They show the Dewisland skyline, Whitchurch and the Preseli Hills, and Penberi, all of which are near the coast of north Pembrokeshire. They were painted in much the same manner as many of Constable's sketches, that is as 'cloudscapes' with local topography. They were all painted 'in the same palette' on a very heavy Bockingford paper. In each instance the paint was applied 'wet on wet', with the initial colour being almost washed out under a tap, and new paint applied, using the difference between 'stainers' and translucent pigment. At the time I quite enjoyed painting in this manner, not least because of the chance element involved in using such a 'heavy-handed' approach. I was very pleased with the results, and in particular with the differences between the skies.

Although I use watercolour when I go out sketching, I rarely use the medium for finished work, mainly because I find it very demanding, and because it requires me to paint at the rate determined by the drying time of the paint, which varies considerably according to the weather. This means that in the winter there can be a longer wait between the applications of colour, whereas in the summer it may be necessary to work quickly. I much prefer to work at my own pace.

Each of the images employs a very low skyline so as to emphasise the vastness of the sky as it is seen in the area. This is because the inland part of north Pembrokeshire is quite flat, so there is no disruption to the view. The northern coast is bounded by the rocky outcrops known as Carn Llidi, Carnedd Lleithyr and Penberi. Looking eastwards from St Davids across the common, the village of Whitchurch can be seen, with the Preseli hills in the far distance.

DEWISLAND SKYLINE

I tend to think of watercolour as being a 'poetic' medium, and after painting these three images I wrote the following piece, hoping that the visual and verbal imagery would reflect each other.

See now the river, brook and pyll,
and the Norman castles, gaunt and still:
and now, the heather-covered hills,
where buzzards of the moorland wheel.

See now where the landsker meets its end,
and where the Afon Cleddau wends:
and now the cromlech and the rock
mark out the land that time forgot.

See now where the moorland and the meadow meet,
where the millwheel drives the tumbling leet:
and now, where the clouds, to heaven soaring,
rejoice in the sound of the great waves' roaring.

See now past the heather and the gorse
where the tiny river runs its course,
to where the light of the winter sun
makes gold the sea where the tide race runs.

The first of these three images was painted from an imaginary viewpoint, a few hundred feet up in the air above the road from Haverfordwest to Newgale, just to the side of the hamlet called Wood. The view of Whitchurch and the Preseli hills is from the lane beside the secondary school at St Davids, and even more prosaically, the image of Penberi is how it is seen when leaving the St Davids recycling centre which is on the A487 Fishguard to Saint Davids road.

It is probably true to say that the image of Penberi is the best watercolour I have painted to date. It is certainly one of the images I very much regret selling.

Top: WHITCHURCH AND THE PRESELI HILLS
Bottom: PENBERI

FISHGUARD BAY AND THE HARBOUR

Fishguard is about eight miles from Plas y Mabws. It has been the location for a number of films, one of which was *Moby Dick*, and another *Under Milk Wood*. The lower town, by the harbour, is very old world, with narrow roads that rise and fall on either side of the Gwaun valley, which opens out to the sea at Fishguard (Abergwaun).

In the first of these four images, 'Fishguard Bay from Harbour Village', I used oil pastel to try to capture something of the way in which even a broad landscape can take on an almost intimate ambience when seen from a particular viewpoint.

The viewpoint for this picture, Harbour Village, is on the clifftop above Goodwick harbour. Looking across the bay, it is possible to appreciate the protection given to the little harbour by the promontory of Pen-caer, ending at Strumble Head.

I do not work a great deal in oil pastel, but when I do so I find it thoroughly enjoyable. I use a very heavy watercolour paper, spirit of turpentine and a hard-bristled brush together with the pastels. Having applied the pastel I use a damp brush to 'scrub in' the colour, after which I will rub off the surplus with a piece of kitchen roll. As with working in watercolour, mistakes made in oil pastel cannot be eradicated, so it is very much a 'go-for-it' medium.

Afon Gwaun runs under the bridge to the right of the second picture (overleaf on p. 51). Now given over mainly to pleasure craft (though the Stena Line ferries sail from Goodwick Harbour, next door) during the 19th century Fishguard was one of the busiest ports in Wales. It was one of three places that the great Victorian engineer Isambard Kingdom Brunel chose in Pembrokeshire as his transatlantic port – though his plans never came to fruition.

This image marks a turning-point in my work and was one of the first I produced where the line does not immediately follow the edge of a painted area. John Piper used this method on many occasions, having first seen it employed by Raul Dufy. I am happy to have continued the tradition although when I have been teaching some school groups, I have been aware that there have been occasions when the teachers do not approve. I therefore take care to explain that painting pictures in art lessons is not necessarily the same as producing a biological or botanical illustration. I do believe that art is something which should be enjoyed by those who participate in the process, and these pictures were enjoyable to produce – as well as, hopefully, being enjoyable to look at.

From the other side of the bay (from where the third picture was first sketched), the folds in the hills are quite beautiful as they seem to climb to the coastal plain before

reaching the Preseli 'Mountains'. In this image I have tried to employ the contrasts provided by the low evening sunlight to trace these geographical folds.

The final image on page 53 is a reworking of the view of Fishguard Bay, from exactly the same viewpoint. In this image, however, I have reduced the three-dimensional curves into two-dimensional planes of colour, producing much more of a surface pattern. Although this image is not to everybody's taste, it was another seminal image because it led to doing another series in a completely new style, with which I'm still experimenting.

FIELD IN WARWICKSHIRE

Until very recently I had hardly painted outside of Pembrokeshire for some fourteen years. One of the rare occasions was when I painted a landscape of a view in Warwickshire, the coloured sketch of which is shown here.

The image transpired as a result of a commission from a Canadian multi-national company which has its European base at Coventry. The company actually commissioned two paintings, this one being my interpretation of the landscape surrounding their European Technical Centre. The painting was produced on two panels at an obtuse angle to each other, reaching 12 feet in length in total. Because the two canvases were so large, and because at that time we were living in a small cottage in Solva, I had to rent a unit at Brawdy, in a disused US Marine base. It was very cold and damp, and I was painting during the period from February to April. Nicola and I would arrive in the mornings and we could quite literally see our breath in the cold air. We eventually installed a couple of gas fires just to dry the paint and provide some source of comfort. I must admit to being quite pleased when I had finished this commission, and could see them hanging in situ, not least because of our discomfort and unconventional surroundings whilst working on the pictures. Producing canvases of that size is quite physically demanding and during the course of the day I believe I clocked up a fair mileage walking to and fro looking at the progress of the work.

The canvases were produced in acrylic on canvas, and I experienced some difficulty in achieving what I consider to be the correct tones. In retrospect, I believe that this was because of the difference in the light between Warwickshire and Pembrokeshire.

GRASSHOLM

When Nicola and I purchased Plas y Mabws near Mathry, the work required to convert it into a home and gallery was to take quite a few months, so we continued working sometimes at the studio gallery in St Davids. The daily journey between the two places, driving along the Fishguard to Saint Davids road, meant that we frequently caught a glimpse of Grassholm. Eventually we were looking forward to seeing the island, with the same anticipation a child has when looking out to sea on a holiday trip.

Like a master of disguises, the island would delight us in the way it would look so different from day to day, depending on the climatic conditions and the time of day. The particular time I chose to paint this picture was at the time when the island wore its spring coat of gannets, turning the distant black rock into a grey and white vessel that seemed to float on the water. It is no exaggeration to say that half of the island is completely covered, and it is known as the largest breeding ground for gannets in Europe.

The dark masses on either side of the foreground are the edges of rocks on the mainland, and the picture was painted as though I had lain down, looking at the rocky island between them.

SELF PORTRAIT

There was a footpath near our home in Plas y Mabws which could be seen from the kitchen of the house. If Nicola were standing by the window, she could see the footpath and the stile which led to the next field. The sun in the late afternoon of the summer months lights up the stile and draws the eye to it.

When I was coming back from a walk one afternoon, Nicola saw me climbing over the stile, and sketched me. When I got back shortly afterwards, she showed me the sketch and we decided that I should try and paint a self portrait using her drawing as a datum. There was one particular problem, in that Nicola sees me as being much younger than I am and it took me quite a long time to redraw myself in a manner that I thought reflected the stiff and slow approach an older man has when negotiating the stile.

It also took me a while to decide what I was going to wear in the picture, primarily because I was actually wearing a dark brown fleece, so that I could hardly be seen in the finished picture. I finally decided on my Liberty shirt which Nicola had bought me the previous Christmas. (If at some time in the future art historians decide to analyse the picture and X-ray my apparel, they will find another three different-coloured shirts underneath).

FELIN GANOL

The village upstream from Solva is Felin Ganol, 'Middle Mill', with its little bridge across the river, a chapel on the side of the hill, and a quarry well-known for miles around for the quality of its stone. Needing some stone for a rock garden, I contacted Alun at the quarry, and my friend Desi brought a few ton to the house with the aid of his JCB. Whilst we were laying it, we discovered one large piece was distinctly different from the rest. It transpired that it was gouged on the sides, and a geologist told me it would have been brought to Middle Mill by a glacier, and had travelled many hundreds of miles. Another friend then told me it was much more likely that the marks were actually made by a plough, and that the differences in the stone were actually only as some were sea-washed and others were not. In either case, it was placed in the centre of the garden as a standing stone.

Felin Ganol (Middle Mill) is a woollen mill in Cwm Solfach, the valley of the river Solva. The walk up (or down) the valley takes in a variety of flora and fauna as it winds to the sea at Solva harbour, which has been the subject of a number of images I have painted.

GARN FAWR

Garn Fawr is an old favourite of mine, and I have painted it many times. This view is from the car park nearby, and shows the two cottages which belonged to John Piper. The one to the right was his studio, and to the left was his 'living cottage', complete with *crog-loft*, a kind of sleeping balcony in the eaves, reached by a ladder. I used to think it was reasonably suitable for John, who was very tall, but I wondered how easy it was for his wife Myfanwy, who was quite a bit shorter.

Garn Fawr is the same rock as is shown in 'Pen-caer'. It can be seen on the northern skyline a few miles from the studio at Plas y Mabws, and is one of a group of rocky outcrops forming a ridge across the Pen-caer peninsula, at the northernmost tip of which is Strumble Head Lighthouse. The peninsula is very wild, especially in the winter, and is quite awesome in the middle of a westerly or northerly gale. Nevertheless I believe that this peninsula is more than partly responsible for John Piper's decision to make Pembrokeshire his base, even though it has been said by others that he came to Pembrokeshire because Snowdonia, where he painted previously for a number of years, became too cold for him.

MELIN TREFIN

This little ruin is on the coast road from Trefin to Saint Davids at a tiny inlet known as Aber Draw. Until early in this century it was a corn-mill, and there is a disused slate quarry and row of quarry workers' cottages nearby. They have been converted into two holiday cottages now. A stone circle sits on top of a hillock, and because of the contours, seems to the passing motorist to appear and disappear by magic on an ever-changing skyline. Although there are still a number of ancient standing stones and circles in the area, as well as *gorsedd* circles in the wake of National Eisteddfod visits, rumour has it that this one is neither, and was erected by the farmer in recent years. Since the original Welsh people pre-date the Celtic myths and legends (many of them Victorian in origin) by a couple of thousand years, I see nothing wrong in a local Welshman creating his own legend, especially since this part of Wales is described as 'the land of mystery and magic'.

The mill at Trefin is the subject of one the nation's favourite poems in the Welsh language. 'Melin Trefin' describes the ruined mill which had not ground corn for many years, even at the time the poem was written by the poet Crwys in 1914. It begins thus:

Nid yw'r felin heno'n malu   The mill does not grind tonight
Yn Nhrefin ym min y môr   At Trefin on the edge of the sea

There is still a special magic to be found in this little cove, and it is a favourite place for local art teachers to take their students, who can frequently be seen sitting around the ruins, industriously producing their images. It does seem a pity, though, that their tutors do not seem to explain that there is more to art than trying to produce photographic likenesses.

DOOR IN FISHGUARD

There seems to be something psychologically special about doors: we can't help wanting to know what lies behind them, or who lives there.

This door is in Hamilton Terrace, Fishguard, close to the old site of the information centre. Fishguard is a pretty little town, much of it being Georgian and Victorian.

The picture is mixed media, in this instance oil pastel, pen and ink, on Bockingford paper. I really enjoy working in this way from time to time, especially using a thick ink with shellac varnish. The image arose from one of those instances when I happened to be in the right place at the right time. Whenever I look at the picture, it is a constant reminder to me of the need to be aware and receptive. I had driven past the house probably fifty times before, but had never noticed the doorway. Then, one day, I passed at a different time, and the sun broke through the clouds to illuminate it just as I was passing on the way from Coedmor to Saint Davids, using the road across Cwm Gwaun.

I painted three pictures of this same door in four years, three of them having been sold, and one retained in my own collection. Each of the pictures is slightly different, because the colour of the door was getting more and more bleached out. A friend told me that it has now been freshly painted, but I have not yet been back to see it.

TENBY HARBOUR

The harbour at Tenby is extremely pretty, and the buildings around it amongst the best kept in the county, in terms both of conservation and decoration. The are nicely coloured, and seem to be repainted every four or five years. This does, however, present something of a problem for an artist including them in a picture, because when their owners redecorate, they frequently change the colours! Multiply that by the number of buildings, and the problem becomes more apparent. Our good friend Toby Rhys-Davies, who was involved in this picture since its inception, has written an account of how it came into being.

I had promised Stan and Nicky I would take them for a walk around the town. I know it quite well because I was born in Tenby, and I already knew that Stan appreciates input from people who are familiar with an area, especially if he intends to use it as subject matter for one of his images. This is what I hoped he would do. As we walked along the prom overlooking North Beach, he said he could see a picture beginning to emerge. We walked back and fore a few times, and Nicola took some photographs whilst Stan did some sketches from different viewpoints.

I left them to it, little knowing that Stan was already working on a major picture, which he was to later publish as a limited-edition print. Nor did any of us know it would be his fastest-selling print up to that time. I thought that Stan would use the sketches in conjunction with the photos to decide which view he wanted to paint. In point of fact he 'stitched' them together to make a semicircular view, which he then straightened out, condensed and rearranged in scale as only he can. The result is an image which people look at and say 'I know the spot he stood on when he painted that picture!', whereas he actually stood in three places, each at least one hundred yards apart. It is his formal training in geometric perspective, together with his ingenuity, which enables him to do this to such amazing effect.

When he came to paint the picture, he did so using his colour/line separation method. When I congratulated him on this, he told me he had developed the idea from John Piper, who developed it from the French Post-Impressionist painter, Rual Dufy. Stan is always ready to acknowledge his influences.

CARNHEDRYN

This tiny hamlet is situated on the main road from St Davids to Fishguard, and when Nicola and I were staying at Coedmor we would pass it when going to paint at St Davids. During that time I found out that John Piper had painted it, yet I could not work out his view. Until a short time later, we were visiting friends, Tom and Cath, at Tretio. As we were crossing Tretio Common, on our way back from their home I suddenly realised where my predecessor would have stood to achieve his view. I couldn't resist painting it from the same place, and also doing some other sketches in the immediate vicinity.

Some time after this, the county council decided to sell the old disused school at Carnhedryn, and I entered into negotiations to purchase it. I withdrew from the negotiations, though, when our surveyor discovered some fairly major problems that would be costly to remedy. Another artist, Peter Daniels, then purchased the property to use as a studio to paint some large mural canvases for a commission, but unfortunately he died before his project had really got underway. The property was then sold again, and is being very nicely restored.

The church, which is also shown in the picture, has been very well converted into a home, with the exterior much as it always was, which is particularly nice to see.

CARREG SAMSON

Carreg Samson is my favourite cromlech. The best known is actually Pentre Ifan, a few miles from Carreg Samson, which is considerably bigger. But Carreg Samson is in an amazing setting, and has its own air of mystery. One moonlit night, Nicola and I were travelling back to Saint Davids, after having dinner with Hugh and Caroline Charles-Jones, where we had been discussing my illustrations for his latest book. The night sky was clear, but there was a mist hovering about one metre above the ground. We took a detour to see Carreg Samson (I had already painted it twice), and it was magical, with the mist floating around the standing stones that support the capstone. I must admit that much of the picture, which I started work on the next day, is from my imagination, but I believe that this particular picture comes closest to the Neo-Romantic tradition. Many local people who saw the original in the window of the gallery before I took it to the printers, remarked that it has the *hwyl*, or spirit. When bestowed by local people this is a special compliment, and I am obviously very pleased to be its recipient.

CHURCH COTTAGE FARM

Church Cottage Farm, Llanstinan, shown in the sketch and painting, is a tiny cottage farm on the path to Llanstinan church to the west of Esgyrn Bottom. The picture was painted from just above the church.

Esgyrn is very marshy, and was, many centuries ago, a huge bog. I believe that it was part of the boundary between two of the ancient Pembrokeshire *cantrefi* or hundreds. When visiting the church, it is necessary to pass through the farmyard and walk down through the marshy ground. In the top right of the picture, the size of the manor house contrasts with the tiny cottage farm with its row of corrugated-iron sheds, like a crooked line of chicks following a mother hen.

When I visited Peter and Susan, who farmed there, Peter was ill in bed, but lent me his Wellington boots so that I could keep my feet dry when walking to the church to draw the cottage. I was told recently that Peter has moved to Llanelli. If so, he could be the last of his family to have farmed at Llanstinan Church Farm

74

CWM GWAUN

One of the most pleasing reviews I have ever received was for this image of Cwm Gwaun when it was reproduced in *The Independent on Sunday*. I hope that it will not be construed as boastful to repeat the reviewer's description:

> The image of Cwm Gwaun is alive with the Celtic greens of the Gwaun Valley itself, seeming to hide the secrets of the times even before the Mabinogion. Stan Rosenthal's latest image is a source of delight, and exudes a poetic mystique.

Of course, the fact that a critic likes (or dislikes) a picture should not be allowed to be the sole determinant of our own taste, but I predicted that the reproductions of this image would be one of the fastest-selling of the limited-edition reproductions, along with 'The Cornfield'. As it turned out, this was not the case. Nevertheless, it remains one of my own favourites, probably because I find it so evocative of the place itself. Having said this, its truth to the actual place might be the reason why the limited edition has not sold out in its entirety. Although very beautiful in its own right, the valley is so dense in places that it could be thought of as frightening to those visitors not familiar with such wooded places.

EAST FARM TRETIO

One particular place that means a lot to Nicola and to me, is East Farm, Tretio. This is for a variety of reasons: not only because it is so pretty, but also because it is the home of Kath and Tom Sutton and their two children, Ben and Ella. Tom and Kath befriended us not long after we came to north Pembrokeshire, and we have spent many happy hours with them, lunching and picnicking, walking across the fields, and doing those things which make Pembrokeshire such a delightful place. Tom and Kath came to the area at about the same time as Nicola and I did, and we share our experiences of the area, together with our love of the local landscape.

It was in this image that I began to simplify the areas of colour, and to use line in a manner distinct from the edge of the coloured shapes. This was later to become a trend in my work, and to develop into a major aspect of what might be called my 'style' of working. I use the word 'style' hesitatingly because I do not like the idea of getting into a rut. I much prefer to keep developing and experimenting. For me, that is what art is about.

FELIN FAWR

One of the little bays on Pen-caer is Aber Bach, where Felin Fawr is situated. Felin Fawr (The Big Mill) was one of many water-driven corn mills in Pembrokeshire, and like virtually all of the others still standing, has now been converted into a dwelling. The garden stretches right down to the storm beach with its shingle bank. Just around the headland is Aber Mawr, once planned as a major port of embarkation for America.

Felin Fawr came onto the market a few years ago, and Nicola and I considered purchasing the property. We opted out when we discovered it was virtually on the high water mark, and that the storm beach (the ridge of stones and large pebbles deposited during storms) had been breeched on more than one occasion. It also transpired that the sea could now be eroding the bank, with no local or national authority willing to accept responsibility for its repair.

The coast path around Aber Mawr and Aber Bach is one of the most impressive stretches of the Pembrokeshire Coast National Park, and Felin Fawr lent itself to being depicted in the same manner as East Farm Tretio, shown previously.

GREEN LANE, MONKS' HAVEN

I have a number of photographs of Graham Sutherland, given to me by a friend whom I met during my time as visiting lecturer to the Graham Sutherland collection when it was based at Picton Castle. He knew that Sutherland was one of my childhood heroes. One of the photographs shows the artist walking along this lane with his wife, Kathleen. Nicola and I went to find the lane, and it was as stunning as we thought it would be, so I painted it.

I have experimented with the image on a number of occasions since, trying to capture the quality and contrast of the distant light seen through the tunnel of trees. The lane joins the church of Saint Ishmael with the little haven at the further end. It passes by the monastery garden, the wall of which can be see to the right-hand side of the lane.

Legend has it that the monks at the monastery baked the bread for some of the castles along the Haven waterway, and there is considerable evidence that there was a large community on the site of Saint Ishmael's.

Virtually everyone who has seen this image comments on 'the light at the end of the tunnel', and it may be for this reason that the limited-edition print has proved so popular.

83

LIME KILNS: THE GRIBBIN, SOLVA

The lime kilns at Solva are a well-known landmark in Pembrokeshire, and are an important part of the industrial heritage of the area. The limestone was brought by sea from the south, and slaked in the kilns, which were situated in virtually every little creek and inlet around the northern coast of the county. It was then used for a variety of purposes, including agriculture and building. It is still used on the fields of Pembrokeshire to keep the level of the soil at the correct acidity for the growing of the amazingly tasteful early Pembrokeshire potatoes. During the last century when kilns were tended by hand, the work was horrendous, and the life of the kiln worker was usually a short one.

The Gribbin, part of the Pembrokeshire Coast National Park, is a promontory at the mouth of the river Solfach. This view is from just above the house known as Woodlands, where Nicola and I lived for a while. The house was once the home of a sea captain, and there was a private right of way from the house down to the harbour, presumably cutting out a lengthy walk for him between his boat and his home. There are many of these little 'cuts' in Solva, and there are still many working boats to be seen, for the shell-fishing industry still thrives there (as it does in Porth-gain, further up the coast).

LUGGER AT PORTHCLAIS (i)

The Dewisland peninsula was on the pilgrims' route from Ireland, and was also visited by Saint Patrick, who, it is said, originally wanted to settle there. Porthclais is probably one of the little harbours he would have used during his own travels, and he would have certainly used a boat similar to the one depicted, as would many of the pilgrims coming to worship in Saint Davids. Two pilgrimages to Saint Davids were said to be worth one to Rome, and three to Saint Davids worth one to Jerusalem.

Boat lovers will recognise the little lugger in the picture as being a picture of a model or toy boat, rather than of a real one. The model I used for the picture was given to me by Anne David, a friend who lived in Saint Davids when Nicola and I lived there. It was made for her when she was a child by the family gardener, and she told us she had sailed it on the Round Pond in Kensington. The whole style of the picture is meant to convey the childlike pleasurable emotions associated with seafaring, fishing and sailing model boats, especially on the Round Pond, an activity I have pursued myself with my daughters when they were children. Perhaps this is why I get such a pleasant feeling when I look at the model Anne gave me.

PICNIC AT SOLVA

'Picnic at Solva' is another of my more experimental images, being in part figurative and in part semi–abstract. In some ways it is similar to the work of the artists of the St. Ives and Newlyn schools, but I painted it in a 'hard edge' manner because that is how I perceived it at the time. When Nicola and I were living in Solva, the view of the pub at the harbour quay is the one we had when we would walk from our home in 'Upper Solva' down the cliff path to the harbour. I painted three of these images at the time, but this is the only one produced as a print.

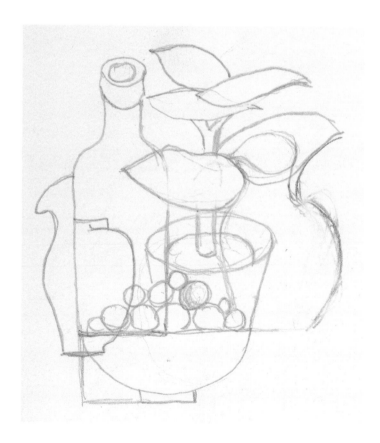

SGWD YR EIRA

This is my impression of Sgwd yr Eira, the amazing waterfall in the Neath Valley. It is one of seven falls in that area, but has the added charm of falling away from the face of the cliff, which is undercut, leaving a footpath behind the falling water. It was used in bygone times by the drovers, to drive their flocks across the river. Although this natural wonder is not to be missed, care must be taken because of the slippery nature of the paths, especially when the falls are at their most picturesque, when they are in full flood after heavy rain.

The whole of the Neath valley is beautiful, but the area where the rivers Hepste and Mellte meet is, in my opinion, the most beautiful of all.

SAINT DAVIDS CATHEDRAL AND BISHOP'S PALACE

The critic and broadcaster Hugh de Loy, who has reviewed a large number of my pictures, said of this one:

> Stan Rosenthal has looked with a fresh eye, the eye of the creative, new beholder, at the vista which John Piper discovered and painted in 1980. The brooding sky in this new image is a wonderful and fitting backdrop to the purple sandstone buildings.

I first saw this view as it was painted by John Piper, and it has always been an ambition to visit the places where he (and Graham Sutherland) had painted, and if possible, to project where their work was taking them. I have been told that in some instances, especially with this one, I have achieved a continuum.

Some artists would prefer not to be thought of as continuing from where somebody else left off, but I believe that if we are aware of the work of others, we all do this, albeit unknowingly. Perhaps the exception might be those who do not attempt to develop from the work of others, but who simply try to copy a style. For me, the joy of art lies in the experimentation involved in trying out new ideas and compositions, and creating new images.

SAINT DAVID'S, LLANYCHAER

This little church, Saint David's, Llanychaer, is on the edge of Cwm Gwaun, the beautiful wooded valley in the north of the county that I had painted previously. Llanychaer church is quite a distance from the village, but this is not unusual in Pembrokeshire, especially when the church is an old one (or on an old site). The word 'Llan' is often associated with churches, but actually refers to an enclosure, such as a stone circle used in pre-Christian worship.

There are many churches which are on the sites of these ancient meeting places, and the pre-historic standing stones are often encapsulated by a wall of the church. They were meeting places in pre-Christian times, and where they are situated away from the villages, it is usually because the priests who chose to live in such churches used them as hermitages, and the parishioners would treat the church as a place to which they would make a sort of pilgrimage.

Saint David's, Llanychaer is very close to a watercourse that runs hard by the disused munitions depot at Trecwn, which has many miles of tunnels built into the rock. At the time I visited the inside of the church, the walls actually glistened in many tones of sandstone. It was very, very damp and eerie, and the yellow and black signs nearby did little to put the visitor at ease, with their statements: KEEP OUT, DANGER OF DEATH, TOXIC and HEAVY METALS. By strange coincidence, the little valley nearby marks the boundary of Dewisland, where many battles were fought in bygone times.

STEAM DRIFTER

This steam drifter is just the same in character as hundreds, if not thousands, that put to sea until recently to catch the herrings, the 'silver darlings' which were eaten fresh, salted or pickled, from Pembrokeshire to Siberia.

My friend Adrian, who works on the tugs out of Milford, told me that the docks there used to have a special landing stage for the herring to facilitate a fast turnaround for the inshore boats that worked just beyond the the mouth of the Haven and around the coast.

Life was hard for the fishermen who put to sea in these steam-driven vessels, that needed almost constant stoking in order to power both the screw and the windlass which assisted in hauling the nets. The little boats, which bobbed about like corks on the water, would put in to port, and leave again as soon as possible. Their catches would be gutted and packed in ice, and sent off to the cities around Britain by train.

Many little boats like this were lost during the evacuation of Dunkirk during the second world war, but there are some which still put to sea, although not necessarily to ply a trade in fishery.

THE BISHOP'S PALACE, SAINT DAVIDS

Much has been written about the splendid Bishop's Palace, its history, its bishops, the changes that led to its ruin. The real expert on the cathedral and bishop's palace at Saint Davids is the incumbent dean, the Rev. Wyn Evans.

Of all the images I painted soon after my return to art, this is one of my favourites. John Piper painted it, and I could not figure where he stood to get his view. Then I remembered something he had said when he visited the art college where I was a pupil over fifty years ago, namely that there is nothing wrong in using multiple viewpoints. Years later I took his advice, and this is the result. I have since used the same methodology on a number of occasions, sometimes using disparate elements, hopefully to good effect. Piper did it in some of the later editions of the Shell Guides.

This particular image comprises three viewpoints in line with each other, as seen when walking along the road from the bell tower towards the deanery.

THE QUEEN'S VIEW

On what may have been her first visit to Saint Davids, Her Majesty the Queen had remarked to a minor canon how much she admired the view from a particular spot in the deanery garden. I knew nothing of this when, many years later, I asked the current dean, the Rev. Wyn Evans, to recommend a viewpoint from which I might paint the cathedral.

He told me of Her Majesty's remark, and showed me the view from that very spot, for he was the minor canon to whom she had expressed her admiration. He offered me the use of the garden to set up my easel, and I painted two pictures from there soon afterwards.

It is the only place where the cathedral, the bishop's palace and the bell tower can be seen together. I gave one of the pictures to the cathedral, and the dean presented it to Her Majesty, so she now has one of my watercolours, painted from that spot, and this picture is from the same viewpoint.

I am told that Her Majesty likes it, and when she visited Saint Davids last year, I was asked to put on an exhibition of my work for her, which I was very pleased to do. As a result, Nicola and I met the Queen, and were invited to a Royal Garden Party, where we also met His Royal Highness, Prince Philip, thereby having two memorable occasions in one day.

The dean believes the view from the deanery is one of the finest in Christendom, and when I heard of this, I wrote the following poem.

For Wyn

When he awakes, the Dean in the Deanery
Throws back the curtains, and looks at the scenery.
"It must be the finest view in Christendom"
he thinks as he puts his clerical collar on.
Then he hurries down the Deanery stairs
To look after the Cathedral and its affairs.

PEMBROKESHIRE CROP and
PEMBROKESHIRE COAST PATH

'Pembrokeshire Crop' and 'Pembrokeshire Coast Path' are two of my pictures that were featured in *Pembrokeshire Life* magazine, where they were described as follows:

> . . . two superb examples of the British neo-Romantic style which especially create a timeless atmosphere. These two pictures paraphrase the subtle nuances which epitomise the eternity of the Dewisland Peninsula.

The first of these two pictures was originally painted many years ago (as 'The Cornfield at Rest Bay, Porthcawl') but in somewhat different proportions. I repainted it recently to make it more suitable for printing as a limited edition. I then painted the second image so that they would work as a pair. They were painted as a tribute to one of my heroes, Ben Shahn, with whom I exhibited many years ago, and who sometimes painted in a very similar manner. The linear parts of the picture are produced by first painting in a light 'undercolour'. When this is thoroughly dry, the darker top colour is laid on a section at a time. Whilst it is still wet, it is gouged out to produce corn, branches, or leaves etc., which show as the lighter colour..

I have subsequently used the technique on a number of different images.

WHITESANDS BAY FROM CARN LLIDI

As with a number of the images reproduced in this book, this picture is taken from an offset-lithograph of an original watercolour, pen and ink drawing of the same size. Reproducing an image of the quality shown here from an offset lithograph is no mean feat, and Gomer Press is to be congratulated on the care taken to show my images to their best advantage.

The view is from the rocky outcrop which rises above the beach at Whitesands, near Saint Davids. The building in the left foreground is the farm where our friends Grenville and Peggy James live. They farm the land around Carn Llidi. In which ever direction one looks, the views are enthralling. Having been born and bred in large cities, when I first walked up Carn Llidi, I found the amount of sky and empty space quite intimidating, but since I have become more familiar with it through drawing it from various angles, and by depicting its more intimate details, I have come to love it, especially as the sun goes down.

The building to the right is Dan y Graig, and the cottage in the middle distance was the home of Moyra Sime, a good friend, whose passing is a loss to us all.

Even the skyline of this is full of history: from left to right are the old windmill tower (Tŵr y Felin), the cathedral tower, Warpool Court, Carn Croeswdig, Clegyr Boia, Glyn Rhosyn and Boncath Rock. The beach is Traeth Mawr, better known as Whitesands.

CADER IDRIS (i)

Lying to the south of the Snowdonia range, Cader Idris is nearly as famous as its bigger sibling, if only for what I consider to be the terrifying walk along its 'knife-edge ridge'. I have not walked it myself, but Nicola has, and took photos for me to work from (although not for the images that appear here).

Cader Idris is amazing, especially for the different faces it shows when seen from its different aspects and at different times of the day, when the sun casts different shadows, altering the appearance of the slopes and crags, as the sketch below shows.

This coloured image was painted in oils, on canvas stretched over board. However, the effect of the technique I used was more akin to watercolour. The paint was applied in thin glazes, each being wiped off almost completely before the next glaze was applied. The colours were applied continuously until the desired effect was achieved. It is a very time-consuming procedure, but is certainly not boring, since each new thin application of colour (using plenty of oil) changes the image. As it nears completion, so the picture unfolds in quite a diffent manner from when other techniques are employed.

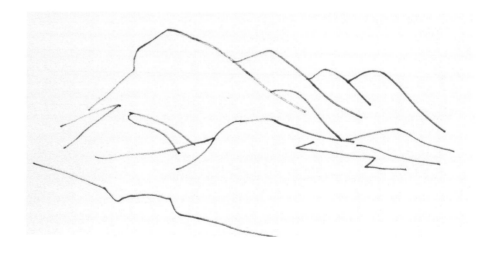

CADER IDRIS (ii)

This second image of Cader follows a style that is proving popular, where the borderline does not follow tightly against the edge of the coloured areas, but is set within them. This is a style of work which was used by Braque and others, including Raul Dufy, who made it better known.

The first time I passed Cader Idris was during the night. About twenty years ago, Bronwen Williams-Ellis was taking a group of us to stay at Wern, on the Llŷn peninsula, and we were in high spirits looking forward to the short holiday we were all taking from Cardiff. We detoured slightly so that Bronwen could point out Cader to us, should the moon break through the clouds sufficiently.

As we approached the point where we thought it should be, I began to think that the sky was getting darker rather than lighter. We stopped the car, and I got out to look. What I had thought to be the sky was in fact Cader Idris, looming over us. I decided to pick some dead grasses (by touch) as a memento, (I collect stones and dried grasses as souvenirs) and as I crept forward to find some, I stumbled into the ditch. I still have the grasses though.

SNOWDONIA RANGE

Painted in the same technique as the first of the two Cader Idris images, this picture of Snowdonia attempts to capture the majesty of the range, which speaks for itself. I have included some sketches below to show various aspects of the range, but the coloured image to the right was painted from the Wynford Vaughan Thomas Memorial.

NEWPORT BAY AND CARN INGLI

I don't put to sea very often, but the thought of what 'Newport Bay and Carn Ingli' would look like was too good to miss, so when the opportunity presented itself to go with a friend in his boat, I took it. The original is an oil pastel, and shows the bay by evening light, with Carn Ingli (the rock of the angels) behind. From the remnants of buildings found there, it is believed that over one thousand people lived on Carn Ingli during the neolithic period, which would have made it quite a metropolis.

Although it may not appear to be the case, I think of this image as one of the first to lead to the painting of 'Solva and St Elvis Bay', and later to 'Porth-gain and Abereiddy', the most recent of my pictures. Although this image is made up of bands of colour, I tend to think of it as linear. At least, it gave me the idea of working again in line, and so took me towards the 'Seven Sisters' image, which can be seen on page 136.

113

PORTHEIDDY PWLL

Portheiddy is a special place for Nicola and me, because it is the west Wales base for a very good friend of ours. Many years ago, when I worked for the Welsh Office, during a lunch break I was with some friends, one of whom had just moved into a very new and untried specialism. Someone asked why he had done so. He replied that having reached early middle age, his previous work lacked some of its stimulus, and the new specialism now supplied it. He recommended the idea of a change of occupation, or at least a variation on the theme, and when my Welsh Office contract came to an end, I took his advice and returned to painting.

Soon after I met Nicola, we moved to west Wales, where we stayed for over twelve years. A few months after our move to north Pembrokehire, who should come into the gallery? None other than my friend Alex, who had sown the seed that started the move. He had just bought a cottage here, and was painting as a hobby.

The little spring is just above his cottage, and it gave me much pleasure to paint it after Alex had pointed it out to me.

SAINT DAVIDS HEAD

I have painted Saint Davids Head many times (see 'Pen-maen Dewi', on page 160) but as anyone who paints will appreciate, each time we return, the perceived image is 'seen with a fresh eye' if only because of intervening experiences and ideas. This was such an instance. Using blocks of colour, I have tried to simplify the image, showing the headland as it appears from the sea, or from the southern side of Saint Bride's Bay. Although different from my more usual style of working, it is by no means unusual for me to attempt this sort of experimentation, although not many of the results find their way into print.

The dramatic appearance of St Davids Head is enhanced during changes in weather conditions. The wind changes direction very quickly during the winter, during which time the westerly storms are quite common. This image shows a south-westerly squall approaching the headland with Carn Llidi being the yellow triangle.

The minimalist composition of this image was part of the development of my more recent work. Although the shapes in this image are angular, and the more recent images tend to be curvaceous and organic, both make use of large flat areas of colour.

SOUTH EAST FROM GARN FAWR

This image is the view from Garn Fawr looking south-east towards Mabws Fawr. On a clear day, our home can be seen in this view, but I spent too long idling when I went out to paint this picture, and the evening brought in the sea-fret, so it is not possible to see anything of Mabws. As though to compensate for this, the lights came on in the cottage at the side of the road and provided a new focal point for the image, making it one of my favourite pictures.

Many people, seeing my more vibrantly coloured images, ask what I do in the winter, implying that the quality of the light at winter-time leaves much to be desired. However, this image hopefully proves that even when the sun is not shining, the Saint Davids peninsula (where it was painted) has a mystery and magic all of its own at any time of year. Although they are damp, the winters in the south-western corner of Wales are rarely very cold, this being because the North Atlantic drift, a tributary of the Gulf Stream, washes the shore with the warm air it has brought with it from the equator.

STORM OVER THE PRESELI HILLS

In the late evening of the 18th April 2000, I was driving towards Mathry from the south when I looked towards my right, that is eastwards, and saw a heavy storm beginning to rise over the distant Preseli hills. By the time I reached the main road immediately below Mathry, the sky over the hills had become a dark purple. I parked my car and got out in order to have a a further look, and as I did so tractors began to appear on the road as local farmers hurried home from the fields in order to tell their families to come and look at this amazing phenomenon. It really was that awesome.

One local farmer invited me to stand in front of his house, which was raised up from the road, so that I could get a better view. I did so and stood with his wife and his two children, watching as the fast setting sun cast its amazing light on a rape seed crop, and on a brown field, which, as though by magic, turned to cadmium red.

For the next few days people were coming into the gallery and phoning up to ask whether I had seen the amazing sunset, but by that time I was already producing this image on a 4 ft by 3 ft canvas.

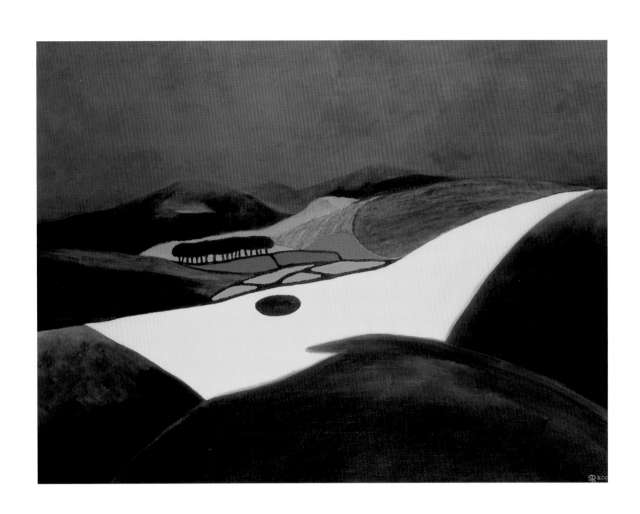

TRELEDDYD FAWR

This little hamlet is tucked into the southern slope of Carnedd Lleithyr, on the Dewisland Peninsula, just beween Carn Llidi and Penberi. Nicola and I used to drive past it each day on our journey from Coedmor, where we lived for a time, to Saint Davids where Nicola had her gallery.

I never saw it as a subject for a painting until we drove past one day at a different time from usual (so that the sun was in a different position, and the light and shade were different), and there was a stiff breeze blowing. Probably because of its movement, I caught sight of the washing on the line. Although I had seen the village on many occasions before, it was only when I noticed the washing that I 'saw' a picture there.

This emphasizes the fact that, as Jung expressed it, 'Chance favours the prepared mind'. It also proves the point that anyone involved in the process of art should try to develop a raised level of sensory receptivity.

The green lane leading up to the left of the picture was at one time known as 'the road to New York', and is mentioned elsewhere in the book (see 'Poppy Cottage').

MABWS FAWR FROM GARN FAWR

Whilst living at Coedmor and working in St Davids, Nicola and I would drive along the A487 daily. We knew that my hero, John Piper, had a cottage just to the north of the road on Garn Fawr which is on the Pen-caer peninsula, and one evening we went to look for it.

All we had as a guide was a photograph showing one corner of the cottage and a chimney with two pieces of slate to stop the down draught. But as we were driving around, Nicola spotted a chimney that looked like the one in the photograph. Sure enough, it was one of John Piper's cottages (we discovered later that he owned two). Walking up to the cottage, we turned to look across that the valley, and it was then that Nicola first saw the woodland and farmhouse that we later discovered to be Mabws Fawr. She pointed it out to me and we remarked to each other how wonderful it would be to live and work in such a beautiful setting. Little did we know at the time that it would one day be ours.

We lived and worked at Mabws Fawr for three years, and it was as delightful a place as we had thought it would be. However, my brain refused to listen to my body, and in my excitement at owning a few acres of woodland, I damaged my thumbs, and then gave myself a hernia. These injuries stopped me from painting for a number of months, and we decided it might be safer for my health if removed from the temptation. This marked the beginning of our discussions as to where we should move. We received requests to move to Kent and to East Sussex, but even though neither of us was born in Wales, we felt we could not leave the principality, and decided to go and live in Cowbridge, near Cardiff, which is nearer for many of my collectors, as well as closer to two of my daughters, my grandchildren and great-grandson, Joshua, and to Nicola's parents.

GREEN LANE, TRETIO

This semi-abstract work shows another green lane, this time at Tretio, in north Pembrokeshire. The rocky outcrops are Carn Llidi and Penberi, and the two standing stones in the foreground are sometimes referred to as the 'mother and child'. There are many standing stones in the area, as well as green lanes such as this, formed by stone banks planted with thorn trees, and therefore known as hedge-banks. Although some of the standing stones are ancient, some of them are recent, having been erected by farmers as back-rubbing stones for cattle. The hedge-banks provide shelter from the strong prevailing south-westerlies.

NORTH PEMBROKESHIRE COAST

Pembrokeshire was home to Nicola and me for over twelve years, and for more than half that time we lived in the north of the county. I believe it is true to say that my work developed more during that period, and in that location, than it did in any other period in my career in art. Of course, other things were happening at the time, so it is very difficult to pinpoint the exact reason for the development, but I'm very much aware that I have been considerably influenced by the changing light conditions, and the variety of shapes and forms that prevail in the area.

This image, I believe, epitomises this variety. Many of my collectors believe it was a turning-point in my own creative development. It certainly marks the beginning of some of the changes I have referred to earlier, in particular the changes from the angular to the more organic shapes.

The picture shows the north Pembrokeshire coastline with Newport Bay to the left, then the promontory of Dinas Head, and Fishguard and Goodwick. To the extreme right is Strumble Head, this being shown as the elongated half-circle capped by Garn Fawr and Garn Fechan.

SOLVA AND SAINT ELVIS BAY

This picture follows on directly from the 'North Pembrokeshire Coast' image shown previously. The overall size of this image is 30 by 48 inches, and it is painted in acrylic stretched onto heavy stretchers.

The image shows the entrance to Solva harbour to the left, with the promontory fort known as the Gribbin facing forward. Next to it on the right is the little inlet known as St Elvis Bay, and beyond it to the right is the wide sweep of Saint Bride's Bay, which is the large bay encompassing the others.

This image was my first large-scale attempt to simplify areas of colour, and I was very pleased with the result. When minimalizing, there is always the risk of going too far, and risking the integrity of the whole. Conversely, not enough simplification can leave a 'bitty' result.

This is actually the view from the coast path, and the original sketch is shown below.

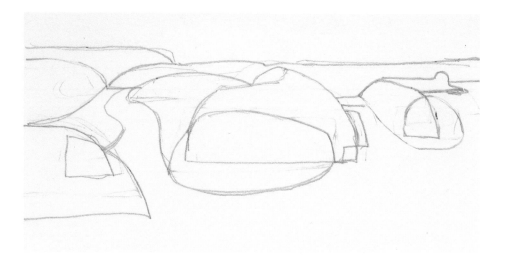

LUGGER AT PORTHCLAIS (ii)

This little Lugger at Porthclais is typical of the little working boats that sailed around the coast of Britain in the latter part of the nineteenth century and the early part of the 20th century. They carried goods, were used for fishing, and were generally the widest used form of transport before the coming of the railways and the motor car. The lug sail eventually gave way to the gaff and boom of the ketch, but the red ochre-dyed sails, frequently oiled with linseed, remained a hallmark of the British coastal trade for many years, in particular on the Thames sailing barges, with their huge spread of sail in distinctive spritsail rig.

I used to see these beautiful boats when growing up as a child in London. For this reason, and because they used to sail around the country to the Welsh ports and harbours, I have included the sketch below, which was from memory.

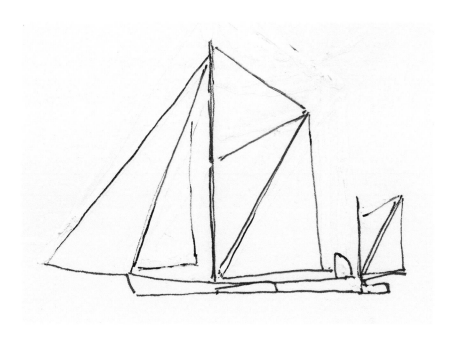

TWO BOATS ON A BEACH

In a similar vein to the beached lugger drying its sails, this image of two little boats on a beach represents a common sight. The cobbles – or sand – form a gentle slope down to the sea, making it possible for the fishermen to wade ashore. I have painted a number of pictures similar to this one since our trip to East Sussex and Kent, and they have proved to be very popular.

I particularly enjoy painting them after I have been working on a picture which requires a lot of cerebral activity, as is required for some images. It is quite likely that my enjoyment is enhanced by the fact that seeing little boats like these on the foreshore reminds me of the time I spent at Southend School of Art. I would walk along the promenade at Southend, Westcliff and to the 'flats' at Lee on Sea, looking at the boats on the mud flats, which stretched out to sea for nearly a mile at low tide.

Sometimes I paint one boat, and sometimes two, but they are virtually always in the same style, simply because it gives me pleasure to draw them that way. It is all too easy to be tempted to look for great philosophical and psychological reasons why we work in a particular way, when the truth might be simply that we enjoy it, or the challenge it presents.

SEVEN SISTERS

I have mentioned this image previously as being one of the first of my return to linear imaging. It is another image I painted on our trip to the south-east of the UK. At one time we owned a painting of Seven Sisters by John Piper, and I often thought it would be interesting to visit the place and paint my own version of a picture of the white cliffs.

We eventually found Cookmere Haven, and I produced the drawing shown below, superimposing a little rowing boat in the foreground, using the style of Christopher Wood, who also influenced many of the other neo-Romantic artists. When we got back home to Pembrokeshire, I produced the coloured image, at first in impasto, and later with the colour generated on the computer, and the line drawn on the print by hand to produce a *remarque* image. I then painted it in acrylic.

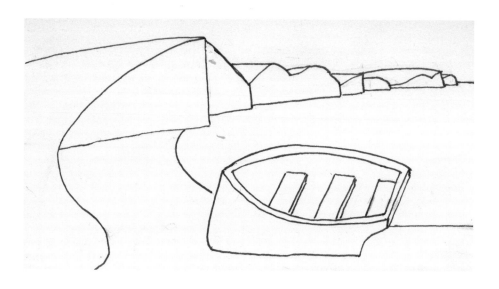

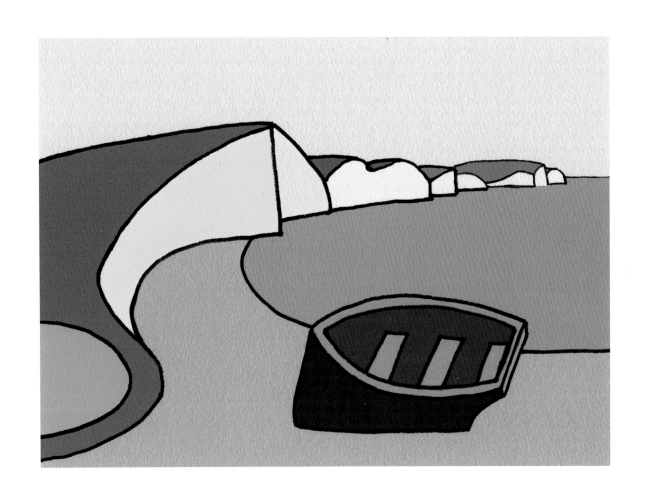

CLIFF

When Nicola and I were in the area of Beachy Head, I was vaguely aware that the cliff looked familiar. I sketched it on the spot from near Cookmere Haven, but when I got home realised I had forgotten to draw in the lighthouse.

Some months later when Nicola and I had visited Cogan primary school, who had made me their adopted artist, we went for a drive along the heritage coast of South Glamorgan, and I then remembered what was familiar about Beachy Head, namely Nash Point, which I had visited when I used to live in Porthcawl.

I worked with line a lot when I was at art college, but had only recently returned to it. It was probably because of my recent work in line, the fact that I was 'thinking in line' (rather than colour), that I was attracted to the sweep of the cliff and the foreground.

I re-drew the image and painted it in monochrome so as not to detract from the strength of the line, using various tones of yellow. The result is shown here.

139

COPSE

This is the second of a series of monochrome images I went on to paint (after 'Cliff'). I had been invited to exhibit a series of pictures in London and at the time I had no idea what pictures I would show. I did not have many to sell (due to my injuries in the woods), but when I had completed the image of the cliff, I decided I should try to paint a series of monochrome images for the show.

The second image, of the copse, was a simplification of another image which I had first painted nine or ten years previously at Cwm Gwaun. When I had first visited the valley, and whilst I was sketching the copse, a man on a bicycle had ridden past, his head appearing and disappearing with the changing levels of the hedge bank. Eventually he rode over the brow of the hill just under the overhanging branches, and disappeared. In my first image I left him out because I did not include figures in my paintings. But later I repainted the image with the man on his bicycle.

Having assuaged my guilt, I now felt able to produce this simplified image without the figure.

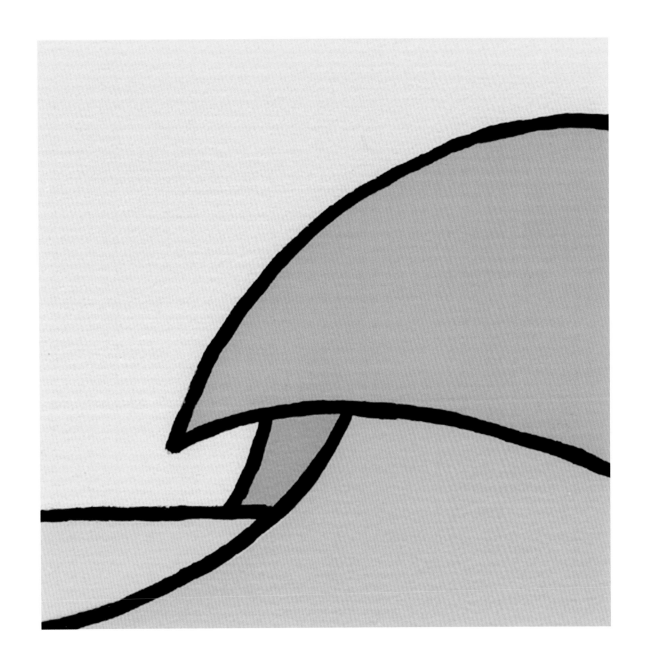

GOODWICK

It was a year or so before painting this image that I had damaged my thumbs working in the woods at Mabws Fawr. Despite a series of injections and various other forms of treatment, old injuries had been awoken and arthritis set in. It became particularly painful to hold a paint-brush to paint anything larger than a few inches square because of the leverage of the brush on my thumb.

Fortunately, by this time, with Nicola's help, I was able to use the computer, and we purchased some extra equipment and some new programmes so that I could work out my initial designs electronically. We then decided to invest in some large print-making equipment, and I began a period of experimentation which is still ongoing.

This image of Goodwick, and that which follows, were amongst the first images to be produced using this equipment as a form of original print-making. Having produced the image of Goodwick, I decided to produce a second image to make a pair, and for this reason used the same palette (range of colours) for each of the images, and ensured that the horizon lines were at the same height in the two images.

The intial images are still hand-drawn with a pencil *plein air*, and are then scanned into the computer. I am then able to experiment with the colour using some of the digital technology which has become available during the past few years. I can also change colours without having to actually paint a whole area, and can experiment without any pressure on my thumb, until I am satisfied with the digitally-produced image, which I can then use as a basis for a painting in pigment-based ink, oils or acrylic.

With regard to the style of these pictures, I was very aware that they differ considerably from the majority of work for which I am known. However, that was an even greater reason to experiment, and I thoroughly enjoyed it, honestly believing I was producing something which was new (for me at least). As the work progressed, I began to get the feeling that I had been here before, not to the places, but to the style. I then realised that I was painting in a manner and style I had first started to experiment with early in my development at art college when I was fifteen years of age, and that the new images had a distinct sylistic similarity to the first two images I ever sold, at about the age of seventeen. I can remember being told by my tutors that they were too advanced at the time, and it was this comment that persuaded me to try to sell them, which I did, for fifteen shillings each. My work then gradually changed, but these two new images are a direct development from those early works, although they do have elements that I have discovered, 'borrowed' and developed along the way during the intervening fifty years.

It was also particularly pleasant to have my thoughts validated by many of my 'original print' collectors, who have expressed their liking for the style, making them the most popular images I have ever created. In many respects, they have validated my theory concerning line, form and colour, because virtually everybody who knows the area around Abereiddy and Porth-gain recognises the foreground as the 'Blue Lagoon' at Abereiddy, and the two landmark cairns at Porth-gain.

I am still working in this style, and it is my intention to go to the Brecon Beacons and to the South Downs to further immerse myself in the luxurious curves of the rolling hills.

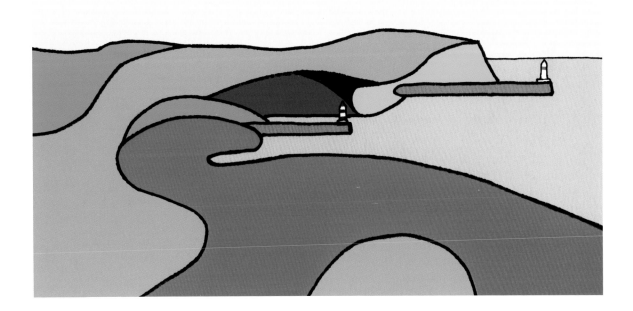

ABEREIDDY AND PORTH-GAIN

As I mentioned previously, Porth-gain seems to have always been a busy little harbour. Shell-fishing still takes place from there, but it is primarily given over to tourism by virtue of 'The Sloop' pub, the 'Harbour Lights' restaurant and 'The Shed' café, which is owned by Rob, a friend of ours. Rob still fishes, and his wife dresses the crab and lobster her husband catches.

Porth-gain was once a thriving port, exporting slate and dolerite to such places as Dublin and London. These materials were brought over the headland from Abereiddy, which is represented in the picture by the 'blue lagoon', which is the cut-out piece in the red foreground. Porth-gain is represented by the two white cairns in the middle distance, used by the seamen to line up their entrance to the tiny harbour. It is so small that even the smallest single well-deck coasters had to be 'warped in' with hawsers.

It has surprised me, but everyone familiar with north Pembrokeshire who has seen this picture recognizes the location almost immediately, even though the view would not normally be seen from the viewpoint I employed, and although the image is a very stylized or semi-abstracted version of the actual landscape. This seems to further validate my theory that capturing the 'quintessential aesthetic' is the most essential part of what I describe as 'the process of art.'

At the time of writing (September 2002), this image is my most recent painting.

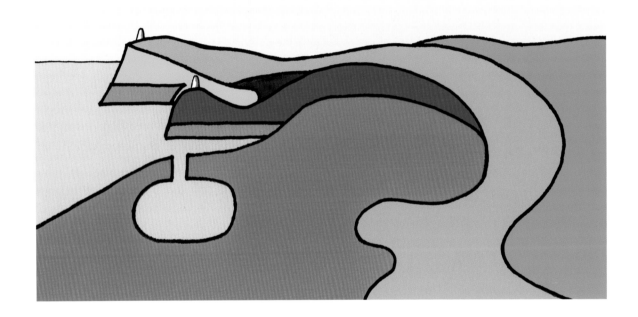

RETURNING

PEN-CAER

Like many artists, I have certain favourite subjects to which I have returned on a number of occasions. For my own part I might return at a different time of day, during different weather or in a different season. The coast of Wales, where I lived for many years, presents itself in many different ways according to seasonal changes and the changes in the quality of light.

Although the winters can be quite wild, even the darkness of the purple skies can be pierced by a shaft of bright winter light. Similarly a summer storm can provide a dark backdrop to a shaft of light picked up by a crop of oilseed rape, the intensity of which is hard to imagine.

I believe it was Heraclitus who said 'we can't tread in the same river twice', by which he meant that everything is continually in a state of flux, and that the river itself is in a perpetual state of change, just as we are ourselves, as we are presented with new experiences. In terms of painting this is no less true. During the months or years which might intervene between the times that I might return to the same place to paint, I will have changed as a result of my own experiences during those months or years, and my style might also have changed, if only because my enjoyment of art is in part due to the amount of experimentation which is available to those who are sufficiently inspired by their surroundings: and the visual inspiration of north Pembrokeshire, where I worked for the last fourteen years, is nothing short of a miracle.

Before living at Plas-y-Mabws, Nicola and I used to drive quite frequently between Cardigan and St Davids, and on the return trip, the headland known as Pen-caer could be clearly seen. One evening we drove off the main road to see how it appeared from a different angle, and found ourselves at Longhouse Farm, where Carreg Samson cromlech stands, and Pen-caer can be seen in the distance. It was a bright evening, and the sky seemed to shimmer with a reflected orange glow, with a few small scattered clouds. With the cromlech in the foreground, and Garn Fawr rising above the fairly flat plane that is Pen-caer, the whole image presented a very impressive sight. In reality the sun was behind us, but I saw no reason why it should not be brought into the picture, since it was the source of the light which made the landscape so impressive. The two white cottages at the foot of Garn Fawr cannot actually be seen from Carreg Samsom, but knowing they were there, and that they belonged to my folk hero, John Piper, I put them into the picture as a tribute to him.

CARREG SAMSON AND STRUMBLE HEAD

The second view, shown overleaf and entitled 'Pen-caer (ii)', also shows the two cottages belonging to John Piper, and in this image, painted some five years after the first, my change in style can be clearly seen. My colours had become more intense and, in this instance, I believe, more dramatic. I particularly like the yellow of the rape seed crop and the undulation of the hills, and the manner in which the road winds its way towards Garn Fawr.

There are many evenings, such as the one shown in this image, when the darkness of night actually seems to fall from above, creating the dramatic effect I have tried to capture.

PEN–CAER (ii)

I have painted the Pen-caer peninsula about six times now, and in the third example, painted last year, more recent changes in my style can be seen. I have shown the two rows of trees which form a prominent part of the landscape when seen from this particular viewpoint, and they appear almost to be silhouettes against the rape crop. In certain conditions, which I describe later, the rocks appear red to my eye, and I have exaggerated that colour in this image to add to its dramatic impact. This is one of the first images I painted in square format. I believe the reason the image has proved so popular as a print is because the harvest lines in the foreground lead the eye towards the centre of the image.

Pen-caer (iii)

JOHN PIPER'S COTTAGES

I have already mentioned my hero, the painter John Piper, who died a few years ago. He has been one of my heroes for almost as long as I remember, and painted a lot in Pembrokeshire. This was one of the reasons that Nicola and I decided to come and live here.

When we discovered the whereabouts of Pen-caer on the map, we went to find out whether we could see the actual cottages where he stayed, and painted for many years. All we had was a copy of a book with a somewhat faded photograph of one of them. Nicola suddenly caught sight of a chimney with a slate 'wind deflector', and thought it could belong to the cottage we were looking for. Sure enough, she was right. We were both very excited, and knocked at the door, but there was nobody at home. Having found it, and since nobody was staying there at the time, we stayed in the area until quite late in the evening, wandering around Garn Fawr, which is behind and slightly to one side of the cottage (In this picture it is hidden by the scrub to the right of the image).

COTTAGE AT PEN-CAER (i)

COTTAGE AT PEN-CAER (ii)

Apparently John and his wife Myfanwy used to live in this cottage when they came to stay, and he used the other cottage as his studio. It was the ruggedness of this part of Pembrokeshire that appealed to him, just as it does to me. I'm always pleased to discover affinities with Piper, (and Graham Sutherland) but I'm not so sure Nicola is as pleased as I am (this is because when John proposed to Myfanwy he warned her that he never took holidays).

I painted the image in acrylic on paper. It was one of my experimental pictures, and seemed to mark a major change in style for me, using heavy lines which do not necessarily match up to the edges of the blocks of colour. John Piper painted in this way for some time, and many people think that this is something I developed from him. Whilst I'm proud that people think I have carried on and developed from where John stopped, the truth is that we both developed it from Dufy and Matisse, and I added my ideas, just as John did before me. We all do it, and that is how progress continues. We cannot help but be influenced by what has moved us, and I believe it is right to pay tribute to our sources… after all, we would not work in the way we do without them.

'Garn Fawr' shows how John's cottage might have looked before he had it restored. It is typical of many to be found in north Pembrokeshire. Seemingly cut into the side of a rocky outcrop, they usually started their lives as quarry workers' shelters, built from the stone of the quarry, into which they 'cwtched' out of the way of the wild winds that sweep off the Atlantic in the winter to give the face of the 'Welshery' its rugged but mystical appearance.

'Cottage at Garn Fawr' (opposite) shows the higher of the two cottages belonging to John Piper, and is the one he used as his studio. He referred to the rock behind it as 'Beetling Rock' but I can find no reference to it by that name. This is painted in the same

GARN FAWR

COTTAGE AT GARN FAWR

palette as the previous image, and they are two images I regret having sold. I have tried to produce repeat versions, but they have not worked as well. In both of these images the sun is an 'imposition' put there for the sake of the composition.

During the past few years, as my work has become better known, various students have studied my work as part of their courses. Some of them have visited the studio to interview me or to study how I work. Most of them stay a few hours but on some occasions they come to stay in the area for a week or so. If I'm not already busy working on an image in the studio, I might take them out sketching for a few hours to show them some of my favourite places. The Pen-caer peninsula is one of those places, and the rock known as Garn Fawr which stands on Pen-caer is a particular favourite. The drawing overleaf shows my impression of John Piper's upper cottage, and I am very fond of the image, both because of its connections with John, and because I believe it to be a particularly good drawing. It may seem strange that I make such comments about my own

155

work, but I do believe that an artist must be able to distinguish between that which he believes to be good and that which he believes has not worked.

The chiaroscuro was particularly strong on the day that I drew this particular image, and although the picture is in black-and-white rather than colour, the strength of light and shade is all the greater for the fact that it is a monochrome.

THE RED FLASH

Pembrokeshire is a peninsula consisting of a number of smaller peninsulas. Consequently it has a very long coastline, and a lot of reflected light from the sea. Pen-maen Dewi (Saint Davids Head) is the western end of the Dewisland peninsula. It is one of those magic places, most of all because of the quality and intensity of the light. It seems that my eyes are particularly attuned to reds, and pick up that colour, even if it is there to only a small degree. This was the situation when I painted this particular picture.

RED FLASH (i)

Although the reds are exaggerated, there is a local climatic/meteorological phenomenon which can cause this effect.. The reason for the title 'Red Flash' is that the pictures are my attempt to capture something of a somewhat rare phenomenon of that name. It occurs at

157

different locations in north Pembrokeshire (and apparently off the west coast of Ireland and some other places), sometimes at dawn, but mostly at dusk, immediately as the sun sets. The effect is to make everything, even the air itself if it is humid, become red, over a range of a few hundred yards.

It is believed to be related to a rather more frequent (but still quite rare) dawn phenomenon known as the 'Green Flash', occurring at the other end of the spectrum. I have never witnessed this for myself because (I suppose) I am rarely awake at that time, but one of my collectors, a retired senior naval officer, told me he saw it many times when on the bridge of an aircraft carrier. Because of the height of the vessel above sea level, the horizon would have been much further distant than is usual, even at sea.

Like most people witnessing the Red Flash for the first time, when I first saw it, I really did not believe what I was seeing. The light cast on a rock was so intensely red that it reminded me of the redness of a child's cheeks when it puts a torch in its mouth. Nicola was with me, and we both knew the other had seen it, but we did not discuss it.

The second time I saw it, I spoke of it to friends born and bred on the Dewisland peninsula. They had all heard of it, and a number of them had seen it for themselves, sufficient for me to mention it to another friend, a U.S. Naval officer at Brawdy (a nearby base existing at the time). He knew it well, and told me that it occurred quite frequently, but in different locations. He knew of many sightings, but referred to them as the 'White Flash' because when they happened, they caused the radar screens to go white momentarily.

It was a relief to hear that it has a scientific explanation, which is to do with 'infra-red saturation', and that many people have seen it. This caused me to look again at some of the work of Turner, who visited the area to paint a couple of hundred years ago. It is known that his vision had a stronger than usual predisposition to certain colours, so it could well be that without being aware of the fact, I was following in his footsteps.

The particular viewpoint for the two 'Red Flash' images is Pwllderi, close to the youth hostel on Pen-caer.

For me it is an inspiring stretch of coastline looking as far down as Penberi and Carn Llidi, just outside Saint Davids. Nicola describes it as 'a place that is quite wild and ancient, left with the exposed scars of ancient eruptions and the terrible power of the land mass being created. It is a place such as this that seems to put our daily lives into perspective.'

The first painting shows the whole Pen-caer peninsula, and the yellow dot on the end of the peninsula is Strumble Head Lighthouse. Because it was the first of the two of these red images, it is usually called 'Red Flash (i)'. The second is a closer view of the lighthouse.

The red seemed to be the most appropriate colour to use as it symbolises the passion and energy that such a special place evokes.

RED FLASH (ii)

I am quite proud of the fact that these two images seem to have been recognised as something of a landmark in their genre. Whatever reputation I have, I believe it stems from these two images, because since I produced them a few years ago, they have been shown in many 'fine art' publications. It has been interesting to note the number of red images I have seen since, namely at Pwllderi and several times at Pen-maen Dewi. In some way I may have helped to awaken the spirit of the neo-Romantic expressionists in a younger

PEN-MAEN DEWI

generation of painters, just as Turner, Chagall, Sutherland and Piper did for me. I was proud when my old and dear friend (and mentor) the eminent artist, critic and historian, Ronald Moore, who died earlier this year, described me as, 'One of the last of the truly experimental neo-Romantic artists'. I am sure he will forgive me if I say I hope he was wrong, and that many others will follow in this tradition.

PWLLDERI

MABWS FAWR

One evening, whilst we were sketching at Garn Fechan, Nicola looked across the valley to the south, and saw what appeared to be a large house half hidden in some woodland. The following day, we found our way across the valley, and discovered that the place we were looking at is known as Mabws Fawr. What we thought was a large house was in fact a group of farm outbuildings, and a largish farmhouse, in use at that time as a restaurant.

MABWS FAWR (i)

MABWS FAWR (ii)

A few months later, as we were driving past Mabws Fawr, we realised that the farm buildings were being converted into dwellings. We went to have a closer look at them, and although the new dwellings were very pretty, we decided they would be too small for us to live in. However, some months later, we discovered that the old farmhouse itself was for sale. Unfortunately, though, it was too expensive for us, and we purchased a house elsewhere.

As it so often does, life took us on many twists and turns until, a couple of years later, we discovered that the price on the old farmhouse itself had been reduced. As luck would have it, somebody made us an offer on the house we were living in at the time, and we calculated that we might be able to afford the old farmhouse after all.

We decided we could not miss out on the opportunity of a such a beautiful old house, and the eight or so acres of woodland which accompanied it.

Mabws Fawr (iii)

The first painting (on p. 162) shows the woods and the house (the building coloured Naples yellow), and the barn conversions, which are painted white. The viewpoint was from the bus stop on the A487 from at St Davids to Fishguard.

I sold the painting, but regretted having done so, so painted the view from the same viewpoint again. I then sold that picture, and painted it for a third time.

The third image, which shows a small group of trees by the river in the foreground, did not work at first but whilst I was a taking off the paint to re-use the canvas, parts of the image remained and others disappeared. Noticing this fortunate accident, I was reminded again of Jung's 'Chance favours the prepared mind'. I then reworked the picture, taking advantage of the accidental changes, and it has become one of my favourites. We have lived at Mabws for 2½ years, but our time there was not always the idyllic life we thought it would be.

Not knowing that we would require planning permission, I started to clear the woods in order to make some walkways so that we could invite collectors to come and spend some time there. We were later to be informed that we could not do so. Although I was very upset, not least because a primary reason for our buying Mabws Fawr was to provide that amenity for my collectors as a way of saying 'Thank you' to them. Strangely, though, the planning decision proved to be a blessing in disguise because by the time we heard it I had damaged my thumbs using power tools, awakening old injuries I had sustained in sporting activities in my youth. As though this was not enough, I also sustained a hernia, and this put paid to my woodland adventure. Unfortunately, the combination of injuries prevented me from painting for quite a few months.

The three pictures shown illustrate the manner in which the same inspirational view can give rise to a variety of styles, and, I believe, also shows how my work has changed over a period of a few years, in the main becoming more minimalist. This is not actually new because I was painting in a minimalist manner half a century ago, so it is more a return to an earlier style which may well be developed further in future work.

FIGURE PAINTING

Although I am best known for my landscape painting, in my early years my strength was in drawing, in particular drawing the human figure. Whilst I do not consider myself to be a portrait artist, I have been told that my figure drawings are recognisable as the people I have drawn because of their posture and 'body language'. I very much admire the portraits by Kyffin Williams, and amazed by the speed at which he works. It takes a very good eye to capture a likeness the way he does it. Also, I admire the figure paintings by the late Will Roberts of Neath, and his attitude to art. He once said, 'If you don't love it, don't paint it!', and I believe he was right. The artist must have at least an empathy for what he or she paints. More even than this, I believe the artist must also love the image he is working on if it is to capture the 'quintessential aesthetic', or as my Welsh friends would say, for it to have any *hwyl*.

NICCI AND BASHO

These four illustrations show examples of figure painting that I have executed during the past five years. The first was an idea for a greetings card which had words around the edge of the image reading, 'She could be seen most evenings, taking her little dog for a walk through the fields because he liked to smell the flowers and watch the butterflies'. The picture shows Nicola walking through some long grass with our dog Basho. He was a very loveable Shitzu. In common with many other snub-nosed dogs, he had some breathing problems, but would insist on running everywhere and so become breathless, as a result of which he would have to stop, sit down and try to get his breath back. One day whilst he was out for his run, he just dropped down dead. Going for a walk is not the same any more, and since poor Basho died I have put on over a stone in weight.

The picture on this page shows four fishermen hauling in the nets on a Brixham trawler. It is my tribute to those seafarers who harvest the seas. When I was at art college I worked two trips on trawlers, and have nothing but the greatest respect for these brave men. Most jobs have an element of risk, but few are as life threatening as deep-sea fishing.

As well as Basho the dog, Nicola and I had another pet, a cat, before my asthma forced us to part with her. Her name was Rimpa, and she was a 'foreign black', which I believed to be a type of Siamese. She was very clever and very demanding. She would like nothing better than to climb up my

HAULING IN THE NETS

SELF PORTRAIT WITH RIMPA THE CAT

back whilst I was painting and drape herself around my shoulders to watch me apply the paint to canvas. She would then lean over and try to knock the end of the brush as it waved in front of her. This picture shows her lying on my lap, preparing to scratch at my jumper. The picture is somewhat unusual in that it is shows the incident as it might be seen from above.

Nicola and I frequently go for a drive to look for new inspiration. On one occasion we went up the coast towards mid-Wales and stopped off at the little harbour at Aberaeron. We bought some fish and chips, and while we were sitting in the car eating them, an old man came around the corner, walking very slowly. He was leaning heavily on his walking stick,

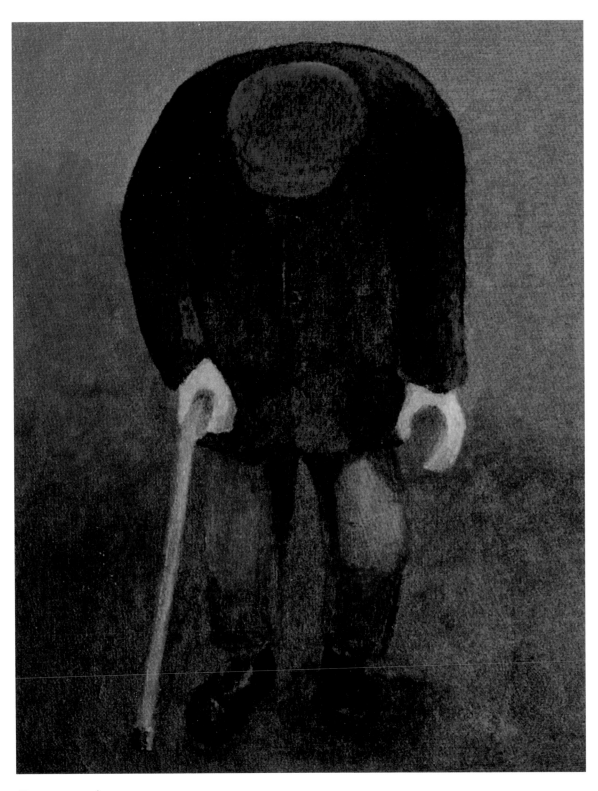

Old man at Aberaeron

and his back was bowed over so that his head was lower than his shoulders. One of his shoe laces was undone, and the other had no shoelace in it whatsoever. He walked so slowly that I had time to hand Nicola my fish and chips, grab a pencil and sketch pad, and complete a quick sketch, all before he had reached us. I painted the picture over the next few days, and admit to being very pleased with it.

THE PROCESS OF ART

For most of us, there are certain episodes in our lives which are so intense emotionally that we lose all sense of objectivity, of time, of who we are, where we are, or what we are doing. Falling in love and the birth of a child are two prime examples of such episodes when the emotion can be so overwhelming that there is total abandonment to the experience. And when the emotional intensity of such an experience is so great that it cannot be contained, it is referred to in psychology as a 'peak experience'.

If the intensity of such an experience is sufficiently powerful, we externalise it. This does not mean that we *want* to externalise it, but that it virtually externalises itself because we are unable to 'contain' it. The manner in which we externalise it is usually immediate, and is physiological (somatic) in the form of laughter or tears (most frequently tears), sometimes described as 'tears of joy'.

When the experience is accompanied by something which can act as a 'trigger' (a piece of music, a smell, an image) it is possible that the recurrence of that associated phenomenon will cause us to 'relive' the emotion we experienced initially. This is known as 'affect recall'. It does not imply that we will necessarily remember the event, nor that we remember the emotion, but that we experience it again, albeit probably to a lesser degree.

In a similar manner, it may be that a phenomenon occurs which has a similarity to the originating peak experience, or which is analogous to it, or a metaphor for it. In such cases also, we might experience the emotion again, possibly without knowing consciously why that emotion has arisen on the new occasion. If the trigger (or 'stimulus') is, for example, a picture, we might say or think, 'That picture really moves me, but I don't know why.'

In some people, a peak experience (or associated affect recall) activates a more complex stimulus than direct and immediate externalisation, triggering the need to create. It is such situations that we might describe as 'inspiration'. It is worth noting that we frequently describe the external world subject (or the 'image' we perceive of it) as being inspiring, but in reality it is not only the image that inspires, but also our emotional response to it at the instant of perception. This is determined by many personal factors prevailing at the time. Inspiration is therefore the result of certain of these personal factors being predominant during an experience, rather than merely the perception of an external world object.

The personal factors I refer to comprise our personal frame of reference. This is the total body of data that make us what we are. It includes such elements as our sense of belonging within a group, as well as our sense of identity as an individual; it includes our value judgements as to what is right and what is wrong, what we like and dislike, how we feel towards others, our personality, and our reactions to our genetic predispositions. The complexity is increased by the fact that various aspects of our frame of reference recede and become predominant at various times, depending to a large extent upon our perceived needs (which may be in reality, personal wants or ego demands) prevailing at the time.

It is our personal frame of reference that helps us feel individual and unique, and through which we recognise our individuality, but because of the ego, we develop a dichotomy between ourselves and others, and between ourselves and the rest of the external world. Also, although our physical existence enables us to interact with the external world, it also keeps us separate from it. Even language tends to create barriers between ourselves and the rest of the external world. All of these factors cumulatively create a barrier that is called 'the subject/object dichotomy'. Of all the factors that contribute to the creation of this barrier, it is probable that ego is the most significant. This is because when it is predominant it prevents us from being receptive to interactive situations (of which peak experiences are but one example).

Peak experiences, like all experiences, are a function of our 'inner world', the world of our thoughts, feelings, memories, ideas and emotions interacting with our 'external world', the physical world outside of ourselves, but within which we exist. If our thoughts are centred upon ourselves (ego-centricity) it is all too easy to miss any interaction which might otherwise have occurred. It is when the inner world is open and receptive to external world stimuli that we are most likely to experience those events that might inspire us. If our long- and short-term personal frames of reference include the need to be aware, to experience and to be creative, the more likely it is that we are open to new experiences generated by external world phenomena, if only because we are more likely to be receptive to them.

The various aspects of the inspiring experience that must be in conjunction for inspiration to occur come from the external world, our personal frame of reference, our receptivity and emotional state at that instant. It is probable that the reason why inspiration does not occur more frequently is that these elements are complex and tenuous, and they must be in conjunction for inspiration to occur. This raises an interesting question: why is it then that some people are inspired (or have peak experiences) more easily or frequently than others? Because so many of the factors I have mentioned are much the same for all of us, I believe the answer must lie in the predominance of the ego. I am not suggesting that artists are without ego, but I do believe that the ego must be in a diminished state, or capable of being over-ridden by other phenomena in order for inspiration to occur.

In my work as a landscape painter, I have come to know many farmers, most of whom are not noted for egotistical behaviour. Although the lonely nature of their work creates a personal frame of reference that does not give high value to communication, I know from our conversations that they are very receptive to peak experiences. Also, I know from the calls I have had from some of them to climb to the top of a particular hill for the most stunning view, or to hurry to a particular place to see an amazing sunset, that their feelings for certain 'landscape phenomena' are as significant for them as they are for me. It pleases me greatly when one of them purchases one of my images to hang in the home, because it is proof for me that I have caught 'something' of what they have also felt.

Just as we are unable to 'contain' the emotion of a peak experience, so, for some of us, there is a need to externalise that 'something' that results in the inner world as a result of its somatic interaction with the external world object of perception. Because this 'something' is triggered in part by what we perceive, I refer to it as being to do with the 'aesthetic' (to do with things apprehended or perceived by the senses). Because it results from the very heart of that experience, I refer to it as 'quintessential'. Therefore, what we share in our experience of an image which moves both the producer and perceiver, I refer to as the 'quintessential aesthetic'.

However, between the perception by the artist of the initiating external world object, and the perception of the finished picture by its perceiver, there occurs a highly complex system of information processing. It is so complex and tenuous and I am so amazed when it occurs that I describe it as being miraculous. This is not because I think of the images I produce as being miraculous, but that it is miraculous that I can produce them, and that any other artist can produce theirs. In brief, I believe that the process of art is so complex that it is a miracle that it occurs at all.

This miraculous process consists of somatically (through the senses) apprehending something in the external world, making that information available to the inner world, where it is acted upon within our personal frame of reference, containing our personal history, our thoughts and feelings, and converted from a percept into a visual concept. We then attempt, through our psychosomatic ability to handle tools and materials, to represent and externalise that visual concept, so that it becomes an object in the external world, standing in its own right as what we describe as a work of art

Furthermore, I believe the most amazing of all parts of the process to be the fact that the information changes its very nature as it moves from one part of the process to another. Perhaps the most intriguing part of all is the disparate nature of this process. A particular scene (for example), is a material object in the 'external world' of the individual, and when we see it through our senses (a 'somatic' or physical function) the information we perceive is transferred to our inner world as a visual percept. The inner world is the store and processor of information, and determines our personal frame of reference, the ever-changing base from which we make our judgements, both conscious and unconscious.

New information is acted upon, and the visual percept then becomes a visual concept (or if our personal frame of reference or some other predisposition has caused us to become particularly audile, and therefore given to auditory conceptualization, it might become an auditory concept, namely a piece of music).

In my own case, if I intend to produce a painting or chiaroscuro drawing, I might simplify the original shapes and forms again on paper, but still using only simplified outlines of those shapes, taken from the photograph and the sketch together. Years ago I would not have used a computer to manipulate the image, but in recent years I have taken to doing so. The manipulation is necessary because I never produce photographic realism through my work, but will usually move things around for the sake of the composition, or to create a new and even artificial viewpoint.

By this stage in the process, or even before, I will usually have a conscious idea (a visual concept) of how the finished work will look. I liken this to the process of composing a piece of music. If we perform in an orchestra playing a piece of music, we are not participating in the same process as the composition of that piece, but in the interpretation of the externalised concept, which is itself a by-product or end-product of the total creative process. Whilst developing the visual concept, the artist is in the role of the composer, but when externalising it in line, chiaroscuro or colour, he is like the performer, or like the composer testing the concept by externalising it. The reason he externalises it is because it is only in this way that it becomes amenable to sensory apprehension (the only way in which it can be seen or heard etc.), and this is how he checks what it sounds like, to determine whether the concept is as he believes it is.

And this is how it is for me: I draw or paint to check out the process as it goes on in my head in the form of electrochemical impulses that whirl around inside our brains, producing something which we cannot describe, but which we become consciously aware of as visual concepts, to which we attach value judgements, thoughts and feelings, thereby increasing the disparate complexity of the concept.

In the case of visual art, we then send other electrochemical impulses through our nervous system to our muscles, which in turn move elements of our skeletal system, so that different coloured paints are arranged as surface patterns in a particular manner onto paper or canvas, maybe using such devices as visual and aerial perspective, and chiaroscuro (light and shade) to give the illusion of a third dimension, greater depth, to increase its emotional intensity, or to create an impression that two dimensions can be representative of three.

And the process does not end there, for as a new object is created in the external world of the artist and subsequent perceivers, the quintessential aesthetic inherent in the perception of that image might move or even inspire others to join in the process of art, and so renew and regenerate the process that gave it birth. It may be that it is a function of art to enable us to relive the instant of inspiration, and thereby relive the feeling or emotion we had at the point of its initiation. If this is the case, then we produce works of art solely for ourselves. However, I would like to think that we show the results of the process to others (or reproduce it as prints) so that others might share that feeling, or 'feel better' for having seen it.

If the latter is the case, then art has at least a shamanistic function, or even as some believe, a spiritual one. Whilst I agree with the first, I have reservations about the second, other than that it might relate through the 'gestalt', which is concerned with 'wholeness', which in turn relates to 'holiness'. The 'gestalt' function is another 'inner world' (or psychological) function, by means of which we are able to recognise whether a chord is 'right or wrong', and by which we might recognise a melody even when it it transposed to another key. In the same way as a chord is perceived in an instant, so too is a picture. We may allow the eye to wander around it, but usually we see the totality first. And in a similar way to recognising a transposed melody, we can recognise a landscape we know, even if the colours are transposed – for example, from green to red (which is something I have been known to do on occasion). Art may well be providing for the perceiver a sense of wholeness which is particularly satisfying or even healing. As my friend the Reverend Michael Robinson has pointed out, holidays are 'holy-days', days set aside to help us 'heal' ourselves, that is, to make ourselves 'whole', and we obtain souvenirs of our holidays to renew that feeling of wholeness. He believes that works of art help to perform that function. Whatever the case, if we are professional artists, we attempt to earn a living by selling the work and sharing it with others as part of an ongoing process.

The fact that art is capable of causing such a vast array of disparate elements to interact with each other, frequently without the conscious knowledge or awareness of the artist who is its catalyst, seems to me to be at least amazing. It was this belief, which first occured to me some forty-five years ago, which gave rise to *Art as Miracle*, published in its entirety in 1993, and which is in the process of being re-written.

Appendix: PAGES FROM A SKETCH-BOOK

The Artist on His Model
(Self Portrait with Ella)

Carn LLidi

ST. NONS

177

Pilgrim with child

The Good Doctor
at Rest

MANDROHON FROM ABOVE TREGROES MOOR

CAERFAI

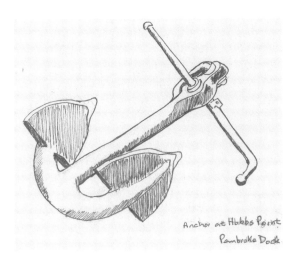

Anchor at Hobbs Point
Pembroke Dock

ACKNOWLEDGEMENTS

I should like to thank everyone who helped make this project possible: the collectors and businesses who supported by subscribing to the publication; my co-author Shelagh Hourahane; the staff at Gomer Press; the artists whose work in other media are shown in the biographical study, namely Mark Walford, Chris Tancock, Rachel Wait and Richard Tong. I also wish to thank Toby Rhys-Davies, the Reverend Michael Robinson, Erica Smith and TS for their comments on my work, and my wife, Nicola, for her photographs and a host of other efficiencies and kindnesses along the journey.

Stan Rosenthal
Cowbridge, 2002

LIST OF SUBSCRIBERS

Rob, Sue, Tom and Grace Doughty
Rochelle and Michal Lee
Steve Fox
County Clothes, Haverfordwest & Tenby
Greg and Diana White
David and Sarah Morley-Davies
Brian and Pam Gilbert
Paul Gilbert
Lynda Reid
Alison Wimbush
Peter Evans
Camilla and Mark Youde
Jane, Gary and Sarah Young
Anita Parfitt and Joseph Titcomb
Bert and Judith Iles
Harbour Lights, Porth-gain
David and Jayne Hamilton-King
Allen Barker
Emma, Kate, Hannah, Ann and Peter Owens
Owen Luder
Debbie and Ashley Grossman
Keith and Jenny Davies
Caroline Fisher
David Hogarth
Maggie Lewis
Mike Nutting
Jane Nutting
Maud and John Harris
Cara and Peter Nicholson
Richard Waterhouse
Dr John Gregory
Anne and Paul Daniels
Stephen Ellis
Hugh and Caroline Fowler-Wright
Anitha Varghese and Ritesh Mewar
Chris and Melanie McGlory
Danielle Mercey
Ruth Davies
Beatrice Davies
Frank Bingley
Arthur, Sue, Mark and Jenny Siddall
Valerie Dearing
Rodney and Margaret Burt
Shirley Green
Sally England
Marion and Peter Bunker
John Skone
Natalie Maclean
Eifion and Julie Evans

Jill and Tom Burt
Tony and Maggie Ayres
Julie Murray
Lesley Jane Haigh
Jon Fairburn
Stephen and Hilary White
Peter, Lisa and Miles Morgan
Carolyn Dexter
John Dexter
Alan Lygo-Baker
Barry and Caroline Tucker
Myron and Esther Luria
Rachel Benson
Terri and Barry Hollings
Evelyn Ross
Jeff and Meryl Dawkings
Jo Grayston
Mike Grayston
Rhian Ellis
Janet and Tony Bushell
Warren Bushell
Truda and Paul Dendy
Susan, Tim, Sophie and Alexander Boag
Myra Boag
Trish Kelly
Mike and Dawn Fairburn
Jo Feeney
Ronald Davies
Rachel Muter
Nick Money
John and Susan Bell
Malcolm King
Phil and Brenda Brooks
Jenny Freeman
Ann Farr
Nicki and Chris Rosser
Kerrera and Rob Briers
Mr R. Schofield
Roger Flavell
Gill and Michael Robinson
Eleanor, Linda and Malcolm Davis
Mr and Mrs L. Blundell
John Evans
Eric Davenport
Sir David and Lady Cox
Doreen and Jeff Charles
Janet George
Maureen and Reg Lowe
Caroline Pidgeon

181

Hilary Clash
Gordon and Katie Goldsmith
Philip Hopper, in memory of my wife Elisabeth
Alex Clapson
Rhonda and David Bedford
Tricia Franks
Samuel Franks
Andrew, Sarah, Charlotte, Jennylee and Emily Bush
Tony and Sheila Ball
Michael Hamill
Jo and Colin Bexley
Sharon and Paul Thomas
Rachel May
Mrs Joan Lane
Mr and Mrs L. G. Chapman
Phillip Norman
Lynne Matthews
Roger, Rachel and Sharon Hulme
Siôn and Michelle Kinsey
Adrian and Helen Reeve
Steve Jacques
Maureen Sheehan
Rob and Liz Jones
Doris Burrows
Wendy Baker
Peter Sheterline
Angela and Richard Barlow
Bruce Hawkins
David and Maureen Jennings
Sue Baldwin
Jo Webb
Andy Warburton
Christine and Steve Maslin
Chris, Jayne and Hannah Woodward
Adrian Bishop
Wendy Evans
Shaun Barker
David and Cynthia Pearson
Keeley Newman-Jones
Maxine, Pav and Anish Isaac Slapper-Alam
Alan Jackson
Mary and Louise Bailey
Peter, Eileen and Matthew Sanham
Rob and Linda Brown
Andy and Sue Pye
Jamie and Sophie Gavin
Paul and Helen Snook
Sue Ellis
Justin Freeman
Bev Priest
Andrew Baugh
Michael Woodford

John Brodie-Good
William and Mandi Griffin
Lisa and Andy Fawcett
Linda and Paul Donovan
Michael and Judith Stewart
Geoff and Hazel Green
Sophie Nuthall
Lewis, Sue, Megan and Sean Gee
Peter and Christine Rooney
Sue Kerry
Dr Sue Powell
Katy Constan
Dr Stephen Baynes
Lyn, Maria and Nia Griffiths
Neil Morgan
Mara Hale
Vicky and Ian Burge
David and Gail Head
Roger and Margaret Head
Drs Christopher and Delia Morris
Pascoe and Irana Elvin
Sandra and Peter Kosian
Ruth Johnson
Jayne Smith
Matthew Wait
John and Celia Dibblee
Pete, Jill, Beth, Mary and Catrin Evans
Mike and Jaz Williams
Eileen Jankovic
Huw James
Fiona Wilson
Giles Kibblewhite
Hilary and Ronnie Marks
Lindsay Martin Hughes
David Paul Dallimore
Mike and Amanda Hopkins
Pat Adams
Michael Beesley
Christine Adams
Dr David Shalom
Helen and Iain Diack
Adam Gell, Amos, Viv, Nick, Dave, Patrick, James
Judith Blackett
Matt and Carol Holdcroft
Alan and Corinna Kershaw
Julia Bamber
Julie, Julian, Tabitha and Isabel Mansel-Thomas
Emma, Dafydd, Bronwen and Benjamin Matteo
    Lloyd
Ceinwen Elias
Mr and Mrs M. Davies
Diane Snee